CAMBRIDGE LIBRARY COLLECTION

Books of enduring scholarly value

Polar Exploration

This series includes accounts, by eye-witnesses and contemporaries, of early expeditions to the Arctic and the Antarctic. Huge resources were invested in such endeavours, particularly the search for the North-West Passage, which, if successful, promised enormous strategic and commercial rewards. Cartographers and scientists travelled with many of the expeditions, and their work made important contributions to earth sciences, climatology, botany and zoology. They also brought back anthropological information about the indigenous peoples of the Arctic region and the southern fringes of the American continent. The series further includes dramatic and poignant accounts of the harsh realities of working in extreme conditions and utter isolation in bygone centuries.

A Summer Search for Sir John Franklin

First published in 1853, this work recounts an unsuccessful expedition to find the missing Franklin expedition. Following the disappearance of Sir John Franklin and his crew during a mission to find the North-West Passage, the Admiralty organised numerous searches for the missing men. The naval officer Edward Inglefield (1820–94) sailed to the Arctic in the summer of 1852 in command of the *Isabel*, a steamer donated by Lady Franklin on the condition that it was used to search for her husband. First published in 1853, Inglefield's account of the voyage is accompanied by a number of illustrations. The work also includes appendices listing the flowering plants and algae of the Arctic region as noted by the botanist George Dickie (1812–82), geographical and meteorological information collected by expedition surgeon Peter Sutherland (1822–1900), and Inglefield's correspondence with the Admiralty.

Cambridge University Press has long been a pioneer in the reissuing of out-of-print titles from its own backlist, producing digital reprints of books that are still sought after by scholars and students but could not be reprinted economically using traditional technology. The Cambridge Library Collection extends this activity to a wider range of books which are still of importance to researchers and professionals, either for the source material they contain, or as landmarks in the history of their academic discipline.

Drawing from the world-renowned collections in the Cambridge University Library and other partner libraries, and guided by the advice of experts in each subject area, Cambridge University Press is using state-of-the-art scanning machines in its own Printing House to capture the content of each book selected for inclusion. The files are processed to give a consistently clear, crisp image, and the books finished to the high quality standard for which the Press is recognised around the world. The latest print-on-demand technology ensures that the books will remain available indefinitely, and that orders for single or multiple copies can quickly be supplied.

The Cambridge Library Collection brings back to life books of enduring scholarly value (including out-of-copyright works originally issued by other publishers) across a wide range of disciplines in the humanities and social sciences and in science and technology.

A Summer Search for
Sir John Franklin

With a Peep into the Polar Basin

E.A. INGLEFIELD

CAMBRIDGE
UNIVERSITY PRESS

University Printing House, Cambridge, CB2 8BS, United Kingdom

Published in the United States of America by Cambridge University Press, New York

Cambridge University Press is part of the University of Cambridge.
It furthers the University's mission by disseminating knowledge in the pursuit of
education, learning and research at the highest international levels of excellence.

www.cambridge.org
Information on this title: www.cambridge.org/9781108071765

© in this compilation Cambridge University Press 2014

This edition first published 1853
This digitally printed version 2014

ISBN 978-1-108-07176-5 Paperback

"ISABEL" ENTERING THE POLAR SEA THROUGH SMITH'S SOUND

A SUMMER SEARCH

FOR

SIR JOHN FRANKLIN;

WITH

A PEEP INTO THE POLAR BASIN.

BY

COMMANDER E. A. INGLEFIELD, R.N.

WITH SHORT NOTICES,

BY PROFESSOR DICKIE, ON THE BOTANY,

AND

BY DR. SUTHERLAND, ON THE METEOROLOGY AND GEOLOGY;

AND A NEW CHART OF THE ARCTIC SEA.

LONDON:

THOMAS HARRISON, 59, PALL MALL,

(LATE JOHN OLLIVIER.)

1853.

DEDICATED

TO

REAR ADMIRAL SIR FRANCIS BEAUFORT, K.C.B.

WHOSE COUNSEL GUIDED,

WHOSE FRIENDSHIP CHEERED,

AND WHOSE APPROBATION

WAS MY AMBITION,

THROUGH HOURS OF TOIL AND HARDSHIP.

INTRODUCTION.

THE Isabel screw schooner, of 149 tons register, was originally fitted by Mr. Donald Beatson, for a voyage in search of the missing ships under Sir John Franklin, by the route of Behring Strait and along the north shores of Siberia. But that expedition, owing to unavoidable difficulties which prevented the accomplishment of his project, was reluctantly abandoned by Mr. Beatson, and thus the Isabel, with five years' provisions for twelve men, and a small high pressure engine of sixteen-horse power, which had been fitted to drive an archimedian screw, besides having been doubled, strengthened, and covered as far up as the bends with galvanized iron, was thrown back upon the hands of Lady Franklin.

This vessel, so well adapted for Arctic service, was offered to the Admiralty as a gift, conditionally that she should be sent upon the service for which she had been equipped; but their Lordships, not wishing to add to the number of vessels already employed on the Arctic search, declined the offer.

A proposal was then made to me on these terms, viz. : that I should provide a crew, and what other fitments the vessel needed, and proceeding to join the Arctic squadron already in Lancaster Sound, deposit with them the provisions I had on board, and return the same season to England ; when, in order to defray all those expenses, the vessel, with all her stores, &c., was to become my sole property.

I had little inclination to be employed
merely as a transport captain, but per-
ceiving how effectively a vessel, so well
prepared in many respects for the Arctic
Seas, might be employed in examining the
hitherto unexplored sounds and shores of
the west coast of Baffin Bay, I agreed to
the proposal so liberally made by Lady
Franklin, but on the clear understanding
that I should be allowed to prosecute the
search on any ground I might think fit,
and in such a manner as I should deem
most suitable to my own views; and provided that I could not only obtain leave
of absence from my Lords Commissioners
of the Admiralty, but that I should be
allowed by their Lordships to finish the
equipment of the vessel in a government
yard, though at my own expense.

Having several times volunteered to
serve in the Arctic expeditions lately sent
out by Government, and being one of

that numerous party who consider that Franklin is to be found, or at all events to be followed by the same path he had pursued, this was too tempting an opportunity to be lost; I sought counsel of several friends upon the subject, but they all refused to advise in a matter where not only my own, but the lives of my crew might be jeopardized, and principally on account of the vessel being unaccompanied, when about to venture upon ground never before visited and totally unknown.

After much deliberation, and carefully weighing all these points, but trusting in an ever watchful Providence, I determined to undertake the expedition—of course contingent upon the compliance of the Admiralty with my request; and upon their Lordships having fully granted all my application, I lost no time in acquainting Lady Franklin with my decision.

Upon the equipment at a Government

yard I had laid particular stress, as I felt
convinced that it could only be by the
exertion I might expect there that I
could possibly hope to leave England in
time to do any thing in the Arctic Seas, as
the season was now far advanced. On the
22nd of June I became the sole proprietor
of the ship or vessel called the Isabel, as
my register ticket quaintly sets forth.

On the following day I formally took
possession, and carried her down the river,
under steam, to Woolwich Dock Yard,
there to be strengthened by the addition of
two iron beams amidships, and thoroughly
overhauled.

The dockyard authorities exerted themselves to the utmost, and seemed to vie
with each other in zeal for the cause I had
undertaken.

I cannot help particularizing the exertions of my friend Mr. Macdonald, the
master attendant, who, though previously

unknown to me, did all that my oldest and best friend could have done towards the full equipment of my little vessel. At this period my time was so much occupied in London that had it not been for his invaluable assistance it would have been impossible that she could have been prepared in the requisite time.

With the engine thoroughly examined, provisions well stowed, sails duly repaired, and ship considerably strengthened, with the addition of sledges, tents, travelling and cooking apparatus, and innumerable articles which my friend found the means of supplying, I was ready to move out of the basin on Sunday the 4th of July.

It is an old saying with sailors, "Sunday sail never fail," still I consider that no work should be performed on that holy day that can be safely postponed; but in this particular case, there were tides to be consulted, as well as the convenience of certain dockyard authorities, and moreover the requisition I had made to the Admiralty for a steamer to tow us forth upon our voyage on the Monday evening, hoping at that time that we should have left the basin on the Saturday. But there was powder to be got on board, and compasses to be corrected by swinging ship at Green-hithe, all of which *must* be done ere we *could* be ready for the tow rope. I thus satisfied my conscience that the work was indeed one of necessity, and so by 6 o'clock on Sunday afternoon we reached the swinging buoy off Greenhithe pier.

The ship secured, I went up to London, to take leave of my much valued friend, Sir Francis Beaufort. This Sunday evening passed away too rapidly. My kind friend thought, I fear, too well of me; he expected too much of my abilities and judgment; but I feel sure in no degree too much of my desire and will to perform my duty.

At the hour of parting I hurried away rather abruptly, but the admiral followed me down stairs, and giving me one farewell blessing at his door, bid me " God speed," and so I parted with one of the kindest hearted men with whom it has ever been my lot to meet.

Monday the 5th was spent in swinging the ship for local attraction, and taking on board gunpowder, of which, with every utensil for its appliance we had been most liberally supplied by the Master General and Board of Ordnance.

Owing to the amount of iron in the vessel, the local attraction was very great. The boiler, engine, screw, its shaft and gearing, together with the iron sheathing, were all powerful agents to bewilder our magnetic instruments.

In an Appendix will be inserted a tabulated form, filled in by my late friend Captain Johnson, after his observations were completed, and from their results he deduced the deviation of our standard and binnacle compasses.

During the afternoon I was honoured by a visit from Sir Roderick Murchison and Doctor Shaw, Doctor and Mrs. Scoresby, and my friend Mr. Thorold, who had all taken the deepest interest in the object of our expedition, and now came to bid me a hearty farewell.

Lady Franklin, the devoted wife of him for whom I was about to seek, with her niece, Miss Cracroft, and several other ladies also came on board. They did not seem to think very highly of my accommodation, at which I do not wonder, as my cabin was only six feet by five feet and a quarter, including table and bed; but they forbore, I could see, to say all they thought. After remaining on board two hours, they left the ship overwhelming me with kind expressions and good wishes for the *dark* future.

At four o'clock, my friend Macdonald came down from Woolwich in the Monkey, bringing some few things of which I had been unable to wait the completion in the dockyard.

Shortly after five, the Lightning, steamer, took our tow-ropes, and slipping the buoy we were soon gliding down the river, at a rate that made us all feel we had been fortunate in obtaining the assistance of this vessel, which had been kindly directed by the Board of Admiralty to take us as far as Peterhead ; and it is with the utmost pleasure that I record here, my grateful acknowledgment of the ready and constant aid that on every occasion I received at their Lordships' hands.

Though the expedition might be for the public good yet it was in part purely a private one, still I derived that countenance and assistance from the noble Duke of Northumberland, down to the lowest official, without which I could not have got away when I did, nor gone forth on my voyage so well prepared and so amply stored.

I was supplied with everything for which I chose to ask, and though it was upon the understanding that I was to pay for it, still to those who are aware of the superiority of the material, and excellency of the work at a government yard, this was no small boon.

Well! on we sped, accompanied for a short distance by my friend Macdonald, who after seeing us fairly off, and requiring no farther aid, manned the Monkey's rigging, and giving three hearty cheers, bid us adieu.

Whilst we are being tugged up the east coast of England and Scotland, I will give a slight sketch of what my views were in undertaking this search of the missing squadron in a single vessel, while so many ships had been employed by government, and were still on this service.

The return of Captain Austin's and Mr. Penny's expeditions, without having obtained positive information as to the route pursued by Sir John Franklin—though indubitable evidence was shown, that he wintered at the entrance of the Wellington Channel, in 1845 and 1846—induced the Admiralty again to dispatch the vessels previously commanded by Captain Austin, under the command of Sir Edward Belcher, for a further search in the same direction; and though this large squadron was increased by a store ship (the North Star), yet it would still require its full force for the examination proposed, and it was therefore impossible to suppose they could make a tour in the direction of Smith and Jones Sounds, albeit a part considered by many well worthy of inquiry, as being one to which it is well known Sir John

Franklin's attention had been sometimes directed.

The west coast of Baffin Bay also appeared to me to deserve more serious attention, for though we may reject the story of the mate of the brig Renovation as to the character of the vessels seen on the travelling iceberg, still it is a part of the bay, where Franklin might have met with an accident on his homeward voyage, and where information might be obtained from the Esquimaux, who are in continual communication with each other, and thus a clue to such a catastrophe would easily be obtained by communicating with them.

My first object was to endeavour to reach Whale, Smith and Jones Sounds by either the eastern or western shores, according as I might find the state of the ice would enable me to do so, and having thoroughly examined these sounds, bays, inlets, or whatever they might turn out to

be (for we have no certain knowledge of
them) I would then, if not forced to winter
in those high latitudes, proceed down the
western coast of Baffin Bay, exploring its
shores as far south as Labrador.

That I might be able satisfactorily to
communicate with the natives, I hoped to
have previously obtained the assistance of
an interpreter, from Holsteinburg, or some
other of the Danish settlements, and to
facilitate this I was furnished with a letter
of introduction from the Danish Ambassador in London, as well as an intima-
tion from Lord Malmesbury the Foreign
Secretary, that he had communicated
with the Danish government on the
subject of my voyage, and requested their
assistance should I be in need of it.

If the lateness of the season or any other
cause should oblige me to winter to the
northward of Lancaster Sound, I hoped
during the spring to be enabled by means

of my dog sledges to communicate with the government squadron, as well as to make a careful search and general survey of all the deep inlets of Baffin Bay, and this, should I be unsuccessful in the great object of my undertaking, would enable me to add largely to our geographic knowledge of that region and to set at rest for ever the much vexed question, of the entrance into the Great Polar Basin through the so-called Smith Sound, which the reader should be aware had never, before our voyage, been approached nearer than seventy miles.

The above is a rough outline of what I hoped, with God's blessing, to effect in the Arctic regions.

Having arrived at Peterhead, I hastened on shore for letters, which I expected to find there awaiting my arrival. On my passage northward, I had forwarded to the Admiralty by a pilot boat an urgent request that the Lightning, steamer, might be allowed to take me clear of Cape Wrath, and great was my disappointment at learning that she could not be spared for that purpose. I then tried to hire a merchant steamer, either at Peterhead or Aberdeen, and would gladly have paid for her service; so essential did it appear to get with all speed to the field of operation. But there was not one to be had at either place, and the necessary economy of my store of fuel forbade my using a pound of it, if possible, until actually on the searching ground.

At Peterhead, I found awaiting my arrival, Mr. Manson the ice-master, who had served in that capacity in Mr. Penny's expedition, Mr. Ogston the second mate, an excellent steady carpenter, and five able seamen, all young and active whalers.

I lost as little time there as possible. A crow's-nest, ice-saws, fresh beef, and a few other necessaries, of which our five days'

voyage had shown us the need, were soon
procured, and on the evening of the 10th
of July, we tripped our anchor, and amidst
the good wishes and cheers of the kind
hearts that accompanied us a short distance
out, sailed away on our lonely voyage—
for my part with as light a heart as I ever
carried from my native shores, putting my
trust in One whose arm I knew would never
fail me, and leaving the result to His wisdom
and goodness.

A SUMMER SEARCH

FOR

SIR JOHN FRANKLIN.

CHAPTER I.

THE crew and officers who formed what the newspapers called my "little band of spirited adventurers," numbered seventeen, and consisted of two ice-masters and a mate, a surgeon, an engineer, a stoker, who was also a blacksmith, two carpenters, a cook, and eight able seamen. For myself, I resolved to have nothing different from my crew, no servant, and my provisions the same, and served at the same hours as theirs ; by these means I hoped to prevent the possibility of anything like discontent, should hardships or privations be our lot.

Mr. Abernethy and Mr. Manson, the two ice-masters, were both well known in " Arctic circles," the former having been several times in government expeditions, and the latter many voyages in whaling pursuits.

Mr. Bardin, the engineer, had been originally engaged for the vessel by Captain Beatson, and having superintended the construction of the engines I was very glad to obtain his services.

Each of these officers, entering fully with me into the spirit of our enterprise, agreed to go at wages much below what they would have received in the government service ; and to each I feel my thanks are due for the manner in which they came forward and offered themselves unreservedly to me in this perilous undertaking.

Dr. Sutherland, the surgeon, having been engaged in the previous arctic expedition under Mr. Penny, and before that in two whaling voyages, was, from his experience in the meteorology of those climes, an invaluable acquisition to our numbers.

The mate, Mr. Oyston, was formerly a whaling master, and had been several voyages to Old Greenland.

Our little Isabel did not of course afford us

very extensive personal accommodation. My cabin was not more than six feet square, having a skylight at the top of a kind of trunk, which passed through a store-room, built on the middle of the quarter deck. My *bunk,* or sleeping berth, was on the starboard side, four feet above the deck, and could only be approached through an aperture in a kind of wooden screen; and certain convenient book shelves and lockers were fitted in all the corners and angles, which none but those accustomed to a seafaring life could have so ingeniously appropriated. A table, two feet by two and a half, was fixed against the bulk-head which separated "the doctor's cabin" from the captain's "state-room;" the former something smaller than the latter, the bunk the same size, but arranged as the sleeping berths of the doctor and Mr. Manson. The engineer's cabin and Mr. Abernethy's occupied positions on either side of the engine-room hatch, so that, when the steam was up, they enjoyed a temperature of a hundred Fahrenheit.

The boiler which was placed as low in the bottom of the vessel as was practicable, lay fore and aft, and was separated from the half-deck by moveable hatches; and the engine, which was composed of two direct action cylinders, on diagonal beams placed like a V, occupied a very small space immediately before the after-cabin, and drove the screw shaft which passed beneath it, by a circular plate carrying crank pins for the connection of the drag-links, with a kind of expansive gearing, which worked by a lever, at once served to set the engine a-head or astern, or by a more contracted scope to cut off a portion of the steam, and thus virtually wire-drawing it. Nothing can be more simple or do better for a high pressure-engine, working continually at forty pounds on the square inch.

The half-deck contained on one side the mess place for the officers, and on the other, the provision store, armoury, and the seamen's library.

From the mainmast, as far forward as the foremast, the deck was filled with provisions of every description, a bulk-heading of patent fuel separating them from the men's mess place. The water in tanks was stowed in the square of the main hatchway.

Upwards of forty-five tons of fuel occupied the hold, and the upper deck was paved with the same material, which completed our stock to about ninety-seven tons.

A large space, forward, was bulk-headed off for the magazine and sail room ; and a store of bread and salt provisions was kept continually on deck for an emergency, ready at a moment's warning to be put over the side, should the destruction of the vessel seem inevitable, either from the irresistible pressure of the ice, or from striking on some sunken rock off the coast ; and the tackles of the long-boat were always kept up and hooked ready for use at the shortest notice.

Fearing light winds in the Pentland Firth, we stood to the northward, and passing through the Roost (as it is termed), took a departure from Fair Island, of which we lost sight at six P.M. on the 12th of July, 1852.

A long swell from the N.W. seemed to indicate that a gale had been blowing from that quarter.

Baffling winds kept us from making much

progress, and on the 14th steam was got up, to urge us forward, though it was most reluctantly that I decided upon attacking our all-important store of fuel ; moreover, deep as we were I could not expect it to add much to her speed, and indeed we only succeeded during a stark calm, in going a-head three knots.

From the 15th to the 17th we spent in struggling against light and adverse breezes, occasionally resorting to the engine.

On Sunday the 18th, I gave out to the people the Bibles and Prayer Books, which had been generously supplied by the Society for the Promotion of Christian Knowledge. Divine service was performed in the forenoon, and it was most satisfactory to see the attention of all the crew to this important duty.

The 19th, we exchanged colours with an English barque bound to the eastward, and on the 20th two more sails were observed working in the same direction. Our observations at noon placed us in 58° 4′ N. and 19° 44′ W., leaving 796 miles yet to run to Cape Farewell.

25th.—Being Sunday, the crew were mustered, the lower deck inspected, and divine service performed, after which I read to the men one of those excellent discourses written for the use of seamen by the Rev. Samuel Maddock. At noon the latitude was found to be only 59° 18′ N. and the longitude 28° 26′ W.

Unsettled cloudy weather on the 26th and 27th precluded all observations, but we tried for soundings with ninety fathoms—no bottom.

28th.—At noon by the sun's altitude we had reached to 59° 23′ N. and by chronometer to 36° 43′ W.

The 29th, a succession of sudden squalls with thick weather during the day, increased to a heavy gale towards midnight, accompanied by a heavy tumbling sea, during which a studding sail boom was carried away and the sail nearly lost in recovering the wreck.

The morning of the 30th broke with a perfect hurricane of wind from E.S.E., the sea washing our decks fore and aft, threatening our top hamper, and washing away some planks and spars that were ill secured on the quarters. At two, the sea had risen so high and the vessel

laboured so much, that I deemed it advisable to
heave her to; the water pouring down the hatch-
ways and flooding the lower deck warned us
of the proximity of the Foul Weather Cape, as
Cape Farewell is termed, vessels seldom passing
it without encountering a gale.

At noon the weather moderated, and we stood
away to the northward, my reckoning and
observation determined the ship's position to
be in lat. 58° 52′, and long. by chronometer,
No. 2185 of Arnold, 43° 17′; or sixty miles
to the S.E. of Cape Farewell. At two, P.M.,
land was reported from aloft, as seen on the
starboard-bow, and going upwards of eight knots
through the water, we soon rose it on the deck,
when every eye was eagerly bent to catch the
first glimpse of the snow-capped mountains.
Towards sunset we were well in with the land.

Bold, rugged, and tempest riven, the coast
seemed to partake the character given by
Greenland sailors to the weather always experienced off its inhospitable shores. A
stormy Petrel flying on board was easily cap-
tured, the poor little creature had lost one leg,

and though the stump was perfectly healed, I
doubt not the want of it occasioned its capture,
as these birds use their feet as a rudder to
guide them in their flight.

By eight P.M., we had sighted several icebergs,
the smoothness of the water, and its low temperature, 33°, now warned us of the proximity
of ice in considerable quantity.

Ere midnight we were surrounded by bergs
and floe pieces, the Isabel, however, elbowed
her way on, pushing rudely aside those pieces
which she could not make it convenient to
avoid, and occasionally striking some sturdy one
with which she had not carefully measured her
strength, and these blows, as we were passing
through the water at the rate of seven knots,
making her tremble from stem to stern; still
on she went, and seemed like myself glad to
have really got amongst her work.

I felt at first extremely solicitous about the
screw, dreading that some of the floe pieces
which had long projecting tongues under water
would catch it. I soon however perceived, that
when the bow struck a piece of ice, it either

received a whirling motion, which would assist
in clearing itself from anything that it might
encounter abaft ; or on the other hand, that
bounding off to a respectable distance, if not
large, it was set by the ripple from the bow,
away on the vessel's quarter; to make all sure
however, I had the screw disconnected, and thus
left free to accommodate itself to any pressure
it might receive from external causes.   To have
raised it would only have endangered it the
more, as it could not have been lifted high
enough to clear the water, deep as we were.

I could not help remarking how singularly
different the character and formation of these
bergs were, to those I had seen off Cape Horn.
The latter being so much more ice-like, and
these appearing as if made out of snow pressed
into unwieldly masses.

About one A.M., Mr. Manson, who was on the
foretopsail yard, reported that we seemed to be
running into a bight in the pack, out of which,
had it once fairly entrapped us, would have cost
hours to beat.   He advised that we should
wear round some loose pieces on our lee beam,

and thus head her off the way we came in—
the hands were speedily turned up, and the wind
leading her away to the S.W. soon brought us
into clear water.

This was my first introduction to the ice, and
glad I was when I found that we had fairly
cleared the stream that had stopped our onward
progress.

The 31st was fine and the sun shining brightly,
we eagerly seized the opportunity of drying the
bedding and clothes which had been drenched
by the gale of the 29th. Two corona were
observed this morning through the thick fog
that enveloped us till the sun had acquired
strength sufficient to disperse it—the outer one
of purple, the inner of a brilliant orange.

Shortly after noon the wind fell, when the
steam was got up and we screwed our way
midst the drifting ice and heavy bergs which
intercepted our path.

Doctor Sutherland busied himself with his
towing-net and found abundance of animal life.
The forms he particularly observed were the
Cetochilus Arcticus and the *Sagita*. *Medusæ*

were very abundant and so completely clogged the net that in a few minutes it was with difficulty it could be drawn in.

August the 1st dawned upon us with strong breezes from N.W. and thick drizzling mist. Whilst working to windward, shortly before noon, we suddenly found the little Isabel running stem on, and within a few fathoms of a gigantic berg; there was no time to wear, and had not she been very ready at stays, a few moments would have sufficed to send us to our long home, as neither the precipitous base of this enormous ice island, nor its inhospitable front, showed a single crevice or projection by which one man could have been saved.

We were, however, mercifully spared from such an awful death, and a short tack to windward enabled us to clear it when we next stayed.

Midst this uncertain weather and dangerous navigation, I was compelled to give up our meeting for divine service in the forenoon, and strong breezes, which obliged us to reef the topsails, kept us all on the alert during the rest of the day.

In the evening, I sent to invite any of the
officers and men who were so disposed, to come
to my cabin for prayers, and I was glad to find
it soon so crowded that it would contain no
more; for the future, therefore, I determined,
when the weather permitted, to have a regular
Sunday evening service on the lower deck.

On the 2nd, the wind becoming lighter, the
steam was got up, and we soon found it a great
advantage, in plying to windward, to keep our
screw at work. The wind gradually freshening,
the fires were banked up, and we pressed her on
with all the sail that she could carry. The
thick weather of the last two days had prevented
our getting observations, and it was, therefore,
charming to learn from the pole star, and from
the moon, on the morning of the 3rd, that we
had advanced to the latitude of 60° 21'.

An Aurora Borealis was observed at midnight
of the 4th, which illumined the whole of the
southern sky with its variegated coruscations of
brilliant light. During the following day we
stood in to within eight miles of the shore, and
it was supposed that we were off Omenarsuk.

We obtained soundings in thirty-five fathoms—sand and broken shells.

Mr. Abernethy, having received a hurt from a tank falling on his leg, I kept the morning watch, and was well repaid by the sight of as glorious a sunrise as ever gladdened the face of nature; the yellow tints of the golden orb shedding their refulgence on the rude and grotesque masses of ice scattered here and there; and the land just tipped on its snow-capped heights by his beams seemed to hail the warmth which would soon send the melting torrents down its steep glaciers, or hurl its frozen masses on the deep, there to be slowly carried to the mild Atlantic, to be dissolved, and to drop their burdens—huge lumps of rock and earth—to the bottom, thus performing nature's endless work of decay and renovation. To no one whose mind is not wholly engrossed by the world and its busy matters can a sunrise fail to lead his thoughts heavenward, and when that is amidst the most glorious and stupendous of Nature's works, how must the reflective man turn his thoughts to the All Wise Creator, whose footstool is the earth, and who "measureth out the waters in the hollow of his hand." What insignificant beings we become even in our own estimation, when we reflect on His Majesty, His Wisdom, and His Power.

Such thoughts involuntarily presented themselves to me, and I rejoiced in the chance which had led me to the contemplation of such a noble scene, as that I now beheld ; heightened as it occasionally was by the hoarse surge of the waters as they rolled into the caverns of some mountain of ice, or by the roar of some other berg while rent in twain with the noise of a park of a thousand artillery, and scattered over the water in showers of fragments for miles around.

Stormy weather on the 5th and 6th prevented our making much progress, and the best thing that we could do was to keep plenty of sea-room ; but all anxiously looking forward to a change of weather, as the lateness of the season rendered it most desirable we should lose no time in getting on our searching ground. The northerly winds might, however, be doing

good in clearing away the ice from the sounds
to which we were bound, and this was the con-
solation we offered each other as day after day
brought us no change.

The 7th proved as threatening as the two previous days, and a heavy sea sadly knocked about
our little barque so that we were glad to see
under our lee some islands, where shelter might be
had from the gale that was brewing ; accordingly
we ran in towards the shore, and after a short
time observed some natives coming off in their
light kyacks. They soon made us understand
that we were off Fiskernœs, a Danish settlement,
and a latitude I succeeded in getting at noon
satisfied me that we had understood them aright.
Having taken the Esquimaux and their canoes
aboard, one of them, seemingly more intelligent
than his fellows, proposed to take the ship into
an anchorage, and deeming it prudent to come
to for the night, I yielded to the inclination I
felt to see the settlement, and to learn a little of
the manners and customs of this northern race
of people. Passing Lichtenfels on the starboard
hand, we shortly came in sight of the little

harbour of Fiskernœs, where, with some difficulty, we anchored in twelve fathoms; but so
very small was the bay, that my precious
little *Isabel* in trending to her anchor struck
with her heel on a shelving rock, on the
south shore, and much to my dismay, knocked
away all the pintles of the rudder. Lucky it
was that this disaster occurred under shelter,
(for an hour's work enabled us to hang the spare
rudder), whereas had the misfortune befallen
amongst the ice, we should have found much
difficulty in repairing it, as the head of the
sternpost had suffered.

Feeling the urgent necessity of proceeding
onward with as little delay as possible, I was
constrained to work all the remainder of that
day and a few hours of the following Sunday
morning, for we found much to do aloft; setting
up rigging, fixing the crow's nest, and making
various other arrangements preparatory to getting fairly amongst the ice.

CHAPTER II.

WHEN the vessel was properly secured, I landed to wait on the Danish governor, Mr. Lazzen. Dr. Sutherland accompanied me on shore, and having presented the letter with which I was provided from the Danish ambassador in England, we were received with every mark of courtesy and hospitality, and were immediately pressed to dine with the family. The repast was served up with wonderful alacrity; for in ten minutes we found ourselves enjoying excellent salmon and venison, garnished with certain fresh vegetables, which were luxuries we had not expected to meet with in 63° latitude. Codfish is one of the staple commodities of export, and we learnt that a ship-load had been carried away to Denmark a few days previous to our arrival.

Though the governor could neither speak nor understand a word of anything but Danish, and his secretary but a very little broken English, I managed to learn a few particulars relative to their mode of life in these regions. Owing to some peculiarities in the ice which were not sufficiently explained to me, sledging is not practised in this bay, and all their carriage is performed by water. Their kyacks, and their light canoes, are principally employed in fishing operations, and a larger vessel, which is called a woman boat (being the only kind in which their women can venture), is used where whales are to be attacked, or fish in large quantities taken.

These women-boats are also employed in carrying the fire-wood, which is collected at some distance up the deep fjords, and is the only fuel on which they can rely for their winter stock. It is a kind of creeping willow, seldom bigger than a man's thumb in girth, and scanty in quantity.

c 2

A few goats supply the governor's family with milk, and his little garden, carefully protected from the winter gales, keeps them in vegetables.

Nothing could exceed his kindness to me, milk was sent off to the vessel with some salmon, and a boat was dispatched into the bay to catch codfish, also to be sent on board. My host was an inordinate smoker, but a fine portly man, and full of a pleasant humour, which kept every one happy around him. The matronly wife was a domestic looking lady, who evidently busied herself much in the culinary process, as her repeated goings and comings with a fork or a spoon in her hand, from her kitchen or her larder, plainly indicated; but it was a right good repast, and we had no business to spy into the machinery by which it had been prepared. Their family consisted of a son and two little daughters, but I was given to understand they had certain other sons and daughters, resident in Copenhagen or elsewhere.

The house in which my friend was domiciled was a good residence, two stories high, the upper part being occupied by the secretary, who thus dwelt within calling distance of his master, along with his small wife and large baby. Dinner ended, I supposed we were expected to retire, as each person rose from his seat, and warmly grasping me by the hand, muttered some words, quite unintelligible to my untutored ear, and then performed the same ceremony all round. I accordingly took my cap, and was about to proceed with the observations I had commenced before dinner, when I was earnestly pressed back again to my seat on the sofa, and entreated to wait till coffee was served. I then remembered the Russian custom of grace after meals, which is performed by each person shaking the hand of every one in company, and saying, "Much good may it do you." Excellent coffee was soon produced, and I was then allowed to go on with my observations in the governor's garden.

The gale blew till sunset, when a calm gave promise of a change of wind, but on the following morning I was sadly disappointed to find it blowing from the old quarter; I consoled myself, however, as before, with the reflection that it was clearing the ice out of the head of the bay and giving us a fair scope for our search in the high latitudes.

The governor, upon learning that I was going to read the service to the crew at eleven, expressed a wish to attend, and accordingly, our work being finished and the ship cleared up, his Excellency came on board a little before that hour with his wife and secretary and all the domestic appendages belonging to each. Upon his stepping over the side, the Danish flag was hoisted at the fore, and a salute of seven guns fired, much to his surprise and to the fright of the women and children. After the salute, we took them below, and then divine service was performed, which, though they could not understand, they certainly seemed to appreciate. The steam being up it was very warm; so having compassion on their frigid temperaments, I dispensed with a sermon on this occasion, and invited them into my cabin to see such European novelties as I had to show, and to give the children some dolls and toys with which I had been provided by some kind friends in London.

Wine and biscuits were offered to their Excellencies, and success to our voyage was cordially drank by them and all present. The secretary, who seemed an intelligent young man, took much interest in examining the engine, and to gratify him, the screw was set in motion and then the steam blown off, to the delight and amazement of the children and the Esquimaux. Having presented the Governor with some cases of preserved beef and soup and a few bottles of good wine, (with which I had been liberally supplied by Lady Franklin,) I allowed my friends to carry me off to the shore, where a sumptuous dinner had been prepared; and on this occasion the secretary and his wife were of the party. Salmon and venison treated in various ways seemed the principle articles of food, and with *soft* bread, butter and vegetables, we fared luxuriously. It would be hard to describe several of the dishes, of which there was such a diversity displayed as would have done credit to a Parisian cook.

Being anxious to witness the forms and simple ceremonies of the service in a native

church, I obeyed the summons of the bell
in the neighbourhood, and soon found myself
in a large, low, whitewashed room, and taking
my seat quietly in a corner, I watched the Esquimaux assembling in this far off land, to worship
the same God and Saviour, that my countrymen had, a few hours before, been praising in
our English churches.

Softly, but rapidly the little meeting-house
filled, and then the door closed, and an Esquimaux with the most forbidding exterior of any
I had seen slowly rose, and with much solemnity
gave out a hymn; and in a few moments the
melodious harmony of many well tuned voices
broke forth. I was delighted with the strain, for
though not a word was intelligible to me, I could
nevertheless feel that each person was lifting his
heart to his Maker, and I unconsciously joined
in the harmony with words which, having learnt
in childhood, now rushed into my mind and bid
me mingle them with the hallelujahs of these
poor semi-savages.

After the hymn, a chapter of the Bible was
read in the Esquimaux language, and then a

prayer, extempore, but full of that fervour and earnest devotion which made me look with more reverence at the ungainly native who was thus leading the hearts of his fellows to the mercy seat of Heaven.

A sermon followed, and then burst from the preacher's lips a flow of elocution that I have seldom heard equalled; without gesticulation he warmed on his subject till the large drops of perspiration fell on the sacred volume, and his tone and emphasis proved that he was gifted with eloquence of no ordinary nature.

Another hymn followed, and then they separated with the blessing of this native Esquimaux catechist—for such I afterwards found he was. A Danish clergyman resides at Frederiks-haab, but he is able to visit Lichtenfels and Fiskernœs only on every other Sunday.

The musical talent of these people was shown upon several occasions. At night they came down to the rocks abreast of the ship and sung some native melodies that were so graceful and full of harmony, that the most cultivated musician might have been charmed with them.

In the afternoon I allowed the ship's company to go on shore for a walk, and Jack seemed to enjoy the opportunity of stretching his legs. Some mosses were collected, and specimens of sea-weed and marine animals were dredged up by the doctor. In the evening having finished all my observations for latitude, longitude, variation, dip, and intensity—and the wind being very light—we had recourse to steam, and on a beautiful evening we cast from our anchors and set forth well prepared to take the ice in good earnest.

Our Esquimaux pilot being at his post, we slowly wended our way among the rocks and small islands which land-locked the harbour, during which the hearty cheers of the Esquimaux women, who could not, like their husbands, accompany us in their kyacks, received from the sailors similar loud tokens of farewell and good feeling. And then on we screwed, surrounded by about twenty of those boats, in which the natives seemed proud of exhibiting their dexterity in throwing the lance, and gliding past each other with wonderful celerity, then

regaining their spears, and sometimes darting
them forward far a-head of the ship. Occasionally they would rest from this exhausting
amusement, and, keeping time with their pad-
dles, they would sing and whistle in parts, their
native glees, which lent a characteristic charm
to the wild scenery of those rude and rugged
shores.

They seemed happy, and, perhaps, that hap-
piness was more real and genuine than that of
the wealthy, whose gold is a source of anxiety,
and whose possessions involve unremitting care.
As the shades of evening closed around us,
our companions dropped off, our pilot alone
remained, but as he also seemed anxious to
return, I rewarded him with some biscuit, a
piece of pork, and an old pair of trowsers, and
he left us.

A treacherous mist coming on, rendered it
rather difficult to get well clear of the islands
which girt the shores of this part of Greenland,
but at length a light breeze coming from the
southward, our studding sails were spread
abroad, we had no further excuse for wasting

our steam, and therefore quickly blew the fires out.

Before bidding a final adieu to the little port of Fiskernœs, I may remark that it forms a very convenient anchorage for vessels that need a refuge from stormy weather ; but the numerous cairns on the adjoining hills and islands are the only guides the mariner has, in conjunction with his latitude, to point out its position; Esquimaux pilots, however, are always ready to push off, and in almost any weather, to conduct him to the anchorage.

There are some dangerous rocks on the port hand going in, which are covered at high water, and some others always above water, on the opposite side, near the town; but these are all the dangers we observed in entering by the south channel. The harbour itself is very small, there being scarcely room for two vessels, and therefore a ship going in with a leading wind should shorten all sail, and rounding to, drop into a berth, letting go her anchor in about fourteen fathoms, and then secure her stern by hawsers from either quarter, to ringbolts provided for the purpose on the rocks. Of the natives I can safely say that we found them invariably honest, they came on board in twenties and thirties whenever they pleased, and we never missed the smallest article.

A strong southerly wind on the 9th and 10th carried us rapidly up the coast, and as I was anxious to keep the shore in sight, lest we should pass Holsteinburg, where I hoped to obtain an interpreter, we kept within eight or ten miles of it; but a thick fog coming on, it was deemed prudent to haul a little farther off, and much to my regret the gale increased so rapidly, that we were obliged to run past Holsteinburg, and to abandon the hope of making it. I regretted this the more, as it was my intention to persuade Adam Beck to join our party, and by a strict search of Wolstenholme Sound with him, to test his veracity in the local circumstances to which he appealed for the confirmation of that cruel report of the murder of Sir John Franklin and his crew, by the natives on that coast.

Having resolved to push for Goodhaven, in

Disko, in order to obtain dogs and interpreters,
on the evening of the 11th, we sighted the bold
cliffs of that island, but the wind falling light
when still fifty miles distant, we were obliged to
get up steam, and yet did not reach the anchorage until five o'clock in the evening of the
12th. The harbour was not easy to find, and
though both ice-masters and the surgeon had
been there before, they were not certain for
which point to steer, in order to make the little
harbour of Lievely, as it is termed by the Danes.

The vast and grotesquely formed icebergs,
which lay grounded off the point, are continually
changing and altering the aspect of the coast,
and hence the difficulty in recognising the spot
that may have been often visited. Luckily we
had been kindly supplied by the governor of
Fiskernœs, with M. Rinke's Danish chart, which
had been recently published, and on which I was
enabled to lay off a course that duly brought us
up to a cone-shaped beacon, painted red and
white in vertical stripes, from which the natives
signalize to each other the approach of whales
to the coast.

So uncertain, however, were we yet as to our being on the right track for the harbour of Lievely, that it was not until a whale boat was seen coming round the point, that we felt at all sure of our position; but a pilot soon jumped on board, and, rounding the rocky promontory on which the beacon stands, and shooting into a little creek at the back, we shortly came to an anchor opposite the settlement, which seemed to consist only of four wooden houses and six mud huts. We did not remain there longer than to obtain a few supplies of which we stood in need, principally sugar and soap, and some plank, that had all been washed away by a heavy sea, off Cape Farewell. The inspector spoke English well, and not only shewed us every attention, but gave me a letter to the authorities at Upernivik, directing that my wants should be there supplied. No dogs could be obtained, as Sir Edward Belcher's expedition had carried off all they could spare. The mail bags of his squadron were found waiting the arrival of the annual Danish vessel, and we quickly added our letters to his dispatches. At six, we steamed out, and pushed away northward with full power. Passing very near the shore, we had a good opportunity for observing the formation of the rocks, which appear all secondary, though granite was seen at one place. Vast flocks of petrels covered the surface of the sea off North East Bay, sitting on the water as far as the eye could reach, and apparently so gorged, that they would scarcely rise as we ploughed our way amongst them. The towing net was put over to collect some of the animaculæ upon which they were feeding, but our speed was too great, the net was torn and we caught nothing.

Muskets were now served to the people, and a target put up at the yard-arm for practice; and I was glad to find that all knew the use of fire-arms, and that some were very fair marks-men. I had a good opportunity of trying the Miniè rifles, with which I had been supplied by the Board of Ordnance, for the vessel being becalmed, a molly-moke, sitting on the water about 350 yards distant, offered a fair object to try the effect of this wonderful weapon, and to my surprise, at the third shot, the ball passed through its body, of which to satisfy myself I had the bird picked up.

Lievely, having failed to produce either dogs or interpreters, of both of which I stood in need, I determined to steer for Upernivik.

Passing along the coast, I made sketches of the headlands, and always accompanied them with angles and one true bearing ; for it appeared to me that faithful views would prove of great assistance to the mariner, in visiting for the first time these shores. Saunderson's Hope is a remarkable mountain, about 3000 feet in height, and forming a good landmark; Svorte-Nuk and Dark Head also are remarkable features.

We observed loons in great numbers here, flying past us occasionally in flocks, or swimming in parties of about fifty on the water. Towards evening, they were seen taking their flight to the rocks, where they roost in holes, high above the influence of the sea.

We found ourselves off Upernivik late on Sunday, the 15th. An Esquimaux came off about midnight (which it must be remembered was now as light as day), and offered to pilot

D

us to the anchorage, and ere long we brought up in the entrance of a little creek, where the Danish vessel was moored some little distance north of the settlement.

On landing on the following morning, I was not long in procuring the dogs and other necessaries, of which we stood in need. Tom and Bella, the latter named after the vessel, seemed ill pleased with their change of abode, and it was some days before they settled down into domestic ship habits.

Mr. Petersen, who had been last year with Mr. Penny's expedition, was living here, and he proved of great use as interpreter to me, in obtaining what I needed from the Danish governor. A description of this settlement would be quite superfluous, for one of these Greenland villages is so exactly the counterpart of another, that any one account of their houses and huts would be equally suitable to all; two or three wooden houses for the settlers, and a few mud huts for the Esquimaux, are the general features of these places.

Mr. Petersen accompanied me on board, and

helped the pilot in getting us out, as we had
taken a rather dangerous position. Assisted by
two boats from the Danish vessel to lay out hawsers and ice anchors to the neighbouring rocks,
we got under way with a fresh southerly wind,
and had not the steam been ready, we should
certainly have gone ashore; for at the moment
the anchor tripped, a strong puff from the
gully off Saunderson's Hope, placed such a
strain upon the whale line, that it presently
broke, and had we not screwed ahead with
full speed, we must inevitably have tailed on
the rocks astern. Barely clear of this danger
the engine suddenly stopped; I rushed to the
hatchway to ascertain the cause, and found the
engineer as much puzzled as myself.

It instantly occurred to me that the screw
must have caught up the rope which had been
carried away, and which of course, owing to
the ship's way, had tailed under the counter;
twenty turns were round the screw in an instant,
and luckily nothing being foul forward, it
gradually tightened, and then stopped the
engine; had a man's leg or arm been in the

D 2

coil, he would have had it neatly amputated with a sixteen horse-power nip. As it was, no further damage was done than stopping the "coffee mill," as the sailors quaintly called our compact little high pressure engine. The wind at this critical moment lulling and drawing off, the jibs were run up, and in a few moments we were clear—a burden off my mind, for the time, almost insupportable.

With regard to the anchorage, it appears to be very unsafe, should the wind blow from the S.W.; the only secure spot against all weathers being the position occupied by the Danish brig, behind some low rocks, where she lay secured between four stout posts.

CHAPTER III.

A STIFF southerly breeze carried us rapidly
away to the northward, and threading our
way amongst a group called the "Woman
Islands," we found ourselves on the 17th
off the Buchan Islands. Numberless icebergs
of vast dimensions, and many of them loaded
with rock and earth, were passed, and often
we were startled by the deafening roar as they
split into a thousand fragments, or reeling and
toppling about, to recover their equilibrium. It
was very grand to behold this gigantic machinery of nature performing with such solemn
slowness the work of decay, and bearing the
massive burdens of rock, torn from their native

soil to a milder clime, where the sun would loosen them from the icy grasp of their adversary, and lodge them in the fathomless depths below. I made sketches and took numerous observations and angles to fix the coast line, but the rapidity with which we passed along prevented much being done in the way of sounding.

A sudden squall bringing us by the lee at midnight of the 17th, carried away the mainboom with a crash that awoke me from my slumbers, with the impression that we had run stem on to an iceberg, and were sinking.

Our excellent old carpenter, Davidson, soon repaired the damage by cutting off the jaws and fitting them to the broken part, thus reducing the boom a few feet in length, which proved no disadvantage. I was very sorry, however, that, in falling, the spar had severely damaged the standard compass, in which I had placed great trust, and looked on it with great respect. The vast quantity of drifting seaweed, which I fancy is torn up from the bottom of the sea by the bergs scraping along in their southward course, continually fouled the patent log, to which I mainly trusted for the distances run along the coast.

On the evening of the 18th we were abreast of the Devil's Thumb, a remarkable pinnacle of land, which, with another known as the Sugar Loaf, form prominent features in the entrance to Melville Bay. The 19th proving calm, steam was got up, and with smooth water we steamed across Melville Bay, which was full of large icebergs, but they did not impede our progress. On the 20th a light breeze springing up from the westward, our fires were banked up, and all sail made. Cloudy skies and frequent mists prevented all observations, and rather puzzled us as we neared a pack seen about noon from the crow's-nest. At first I was doubtful whether it would not be best at once to dash in, and press through it to Cape York, but the ice-masters carefully looked out for a lane, and we succeeded, about a mile and a half to the east-ward, in getting into a fine opening, which gave every prospect of leading us into open water.

We had not long been struggling with the loose ice when a great bear came close down to the ship to inquire our business ; I saluted him with a shot from "*the* rifle," but not striking him in a vital part he made off, and our efforts to follow him in the whale-boat proved fruitless. I was sorry to leave the poor brute so badly wounded, and my dogs were as much in need of the flesh as I was of the skin, to fulfil some of the promises I made to my friends on leaving England.

Having succeeded in passing through the pack, and in reaching the open water, we pushed eagerly on ; while the sun bursting forth dispelled the mist, and gladdening our hearts amidst the solitude of ice and snow, rapidly thawed the latter that lay on our decks and yards after a morning shower, which, though slight, had covered them.

Forty-one days only have elapsed since we tripped anchor from Peterhead, and here we are in Melville Bay, three days later only (as regards the period of the season) than the Penny Expedition of last year, with apparently a far better season, and in a vessel unencumbered with a consort or with any orders.

A clear sky and a tolerable horizon enabled me to obtain a good azimuth, which gave the variation 88° 19′ W.; but I had no means of ascertaining the deviation due to local attraction, though I endeavoured to allow a proportionate increase to that which was observed at Greenhithe where the ship was swung previous to her departure.

We now kept the steam continually up, ready for any emergency, as the slight expenditure necessary for banking up was not to be weighed against the advantage of having this all-powerful agent ready at a quarter of an hour's call.

At last, the long-wished-for Cape York hoved in sight—Bushnan Island on the lee beam, and the Crimson Cliffs and Cape Dudley Digges stretching far away to the northward. The coast *seemed* tolerably free from ice, though gigantic bergs were seen here and there, like "grim watchmen" of the bay, scowling on the adventurous stranger who would tempt those dread shores which had witnessed the destruction of

many a fine vessel, and which, as we afterwards
learnt, had been the scene of the total loss
of two fine whalers but a few weeks before our
arrival.

We kept the whale-boat always ready, with a
week's provisions, so that she might be detached
at a moment's notice, and not be distressed
for two or three days should any difficulty occur
in returning.

At four A.M. of the 21st we were well up with
the loose ice, which was lying off Cape York ;
and as I found it would be impossible to get
near enough to the shore to look out for any
natives, with whom it was very desirable to
communicate, we pushed boldly in, and soon
commenced thumping our way along in the
narrow lanes as they presented themselves.
A wedge of a ship's mast, a cask, a cork,
and some staves were picked up, and at the
time appeared to be well worthy of our notice
with reference to the missing squadron, but the
disasters of the whalers in Melville Bay (which
we learnt on our arrival at Beechey Island) accounted for the presence of these articles.

KILLING A BEAR OFF CAPE YORK

Whilst working our way amongst this ice, a
bear was observed from the crow's-nest, swimming amongst the loose pieces. A boat was
lowered and I proceeded in pursuit, but Bruin
swam hard for his life, and we did not succeed
in coming up with him, till we were some
distance from the ship. A shot I put into him
with the Miniè rifle rendered him desperate,
and he turned upon me, swimming and plunging
over the brash ice to get at the boat; but the
rifle had been discharged and was not prepared
for a second shot, and we had not provided
ourselves with an axe, a very necessary weapon
to prevent these brutes from getting into the
boat, which they always attempt to do when
badly hurt. I was, however, otherwise prepared
for my shaggy enemy, who roaring and blowing
as he advanced, whispered desperate things to
those who were not cognizant of my resources.
He came within a single yard, when a Colt's
revolver was pulled from my breast-coat pocket,
and waiting till his nose nearly touched the
muzzle—Bruin lay dead—his head falling between his fore-legs—and we quietly towed
him alongside.

He proved a fine young fellow, with an excellent coat, and his arrival was joyfully welcomed
by my famishing dogs, whose stomachs had
hardly accustomed themselves to the scraps
of meat, biscuit, and remains of pea-soup,
upon which we had been forced to feed them.
The bear was scarcely hoisted in, when another
was seen, and though the vessel was in anything
but a comfortable position, surrounded as she was
by thick heavy ice, and too near the land, still
I could not resist the temptation, and away we
went after the beast, who was much larger, and
we thought might, therefore, shew more sport.

Mr. Bardin, the engineer was looking very
wistfully over the side as I stepped into the
boat, and knowing he was as fond of adventure
as myself, I invited him to the onslaught; he
came, but only to be disappointed, for the first
shot from my Miniè rifle saved Bruin from the
necessity of seeking for any more seals. He too
was soon safely lodged on board, when, hoisting
up the boat we proceeded onward, determined not
to allow any more bears to distract our attention.

Dr. Sutherland succeeded in getting his
dredge down to fifty fathoms, at about two

miles distance from the land, and was rewarded
by bringing to the surface what he considered
a very fine *ascidium*. The cliffs were now
covered with snow, and every thing seemed
putting on the dreary garb of winter. I felt
sure, and indeed I was warned by the ice-
masters, that we must soon prepare ourselves
for winter, and accordingly all the water which
I supposed we should not require before the
event of freezing-in took place, was pumped
out of the tanks, and our attention was turned to
looking for some place that might be suitable for
winter quarters. The Beverly Cliffs, spoken of by
Ross as the Crimson Cliffs, were, I presume, not
expecting visitors so late in the year; for they
were quite unattired in their gorgeous clothing.
A red or rather orange coloured lichen, (*Leca-
nora elegans*), grew rather abundantly on the
rocks, but I was told by the doctor, who had
seen the crimson snow, that this is not the
cause of the curious tinge it assumes.

The 22nd proved rather a boisterous day, and
the wind veering to the northward, obliged us
to bank up the fires, and take to our canvas while

beating to windward, amongst the stupendous bergs that lay near Conical Island. An extra- ordinary spot of granitic formation, and com- posed of a number of peaked masses which seemed piled in rude confusion over each other ; angles, sketches, and bearings, were taken to fix, with more exactitude, the coast line of these rarely visited shores. A good latitude at noon, 76° 10', longitude 68° 50', gave a base point for our angles, and I hoped the matter I collected, might prove useful to the hydrography of this ill laid down gulf.

Becalmed towards the evening, we drifted tolerably close to the great glacier of Petowak, and not liking our position, surrounded as we were by stupendous bergs, one hundred and eighty of which had been counted from the crow's-nest, I ordered steam to be got up. In the mean time voices were heard shouting from the shore, and soon Esquimaux were observed coming down the face of the glacier, in an adjoining ravine ; they seemed most anxious we should communicate with them, and I was equally willing for the visit; the whale-boat was

prepared, and in making our way amongst the
brash ice, which lay off the shore, I was sorry
to observe that in every still spot bay ice immediately formed; the certain harbinger of winter.
This glacier of Petowak is a wonderful work of
nature, extending as it does, upwards of a mile
into the sea, and four or five miles inland, with
a smooth unbroken surface; it carries one's
thoughts back to the age when this gigantic ice
formation was in its infancy; and when, during
the summer months, it was possibly but a little
purling stream, at the head of a deep bay.

Glaciers are the manufactories, if I might
so say, of ice-bergs, and the vast reservoirs from
whence proceed these wondrous ice-islands. The
action of the sea, and more moderate temperature of the water at the foot of the glacier,
cause great pieces of ice to be dislodged, which
slipping off the parent stock, are launched forth,
to be carried south by winds and tides, till a
milder climate, melting their sides, (which I
have seen occasionally pouring forth a torrent of
water), mingles the mass with the mighty deep.

Upon approaching a little sandy bay near

which the natives seemed waiting our arrival
with some anxiety, I observed that they consulted awhile and then scampered off, and it
was not till I had assured them with the sign of
peace, holding both arms high above the head,
and shouting to them words, accepted by all the
tribes of Esquimaux as, signifying " Peace, we
are friends," that they could be induced to return.
Upon landing I shook them by the hand and
gave some small presents to their wives and
children, which re-assuring them, they commenced the most boisterous laughter and curious
examination of our boat and clothing. I am
convinced from the manner in which they
laughed at our appearance and their timidity at
our first approach that they had never before
beheld Europeans.

We endeavoured to learn from them where to
find the village of Omenak, and an old woman
very intelligibly drew on the snow with a stone
an outline of the coast, placing her finger on the
position of Omenak, but I could not persuade
any one of them to accompany us, and, therefore,
was obliged to content myself, after making a

few general inquiries among the individuals
with carrying off various specimens of the rocks
and indigenous plants. These people were
clothed in bear, fox, reindeer, and seal skins;
they seemed in the most robust health, and
some of them had rotches, small sea birds in
their hands which they had evidently been collecting amongst the rocks. These birds are very
delicious eating, and may be collected in thousands during the spring when they resort to the
cliffs to breed.

Nothing of European ware was found with
these natives, nor were kyacks seen; indeed, I
am inclined to believe, that like the natives seen
last year at Cape York, their habits are those of
the hunter and not of the fisherman. A hand-
kerchief with a portrait of our gracious Queen
in the centre attracted much attention; and as
we pulled away from the shore, I observed them,
with it spread out on the snow, examining it
in all positions with apparent awe.

With a light southerly wind and clear sky,
we steamed away towards Cape Atholl, passing
inside of a low rock that lies about a mile and a

E

half off the shore, and which, I should suppose, is covered in spring tides. How I longed for time to survey this coast! The chart was so incorrect that I was compelled to trust to my wits, and every opportunity was embraced for getting observations and angles to fix its outline more exactly. The wind heading as we approached Cape Atholl, we were obliged to ply under steam and sail to windward, and before 8 A.M. of the morning of the 23rd, we were well inside the point. Whilst aloft in the crow's-nest at four o'clock this morning, observing something floating behind a piece of ice, which attracting my attention, I hurried down, and immediately lowering one of the light boats, went, with one other hand, to examine it, and found it to be a part of a ship's deck with a heavy piece of iron bolted firmly to it. Long afterwards we learned that it must have been part of the American whaler that was lost in Melville Bay, but at the time it attracted a good deal of our attention, and excited no little interest in people eagerly searching for information of any kind.

The strong northerly current along this shore is well shown by the above circumstance; and yet be it remembered that we had experienced heavy gales from the northward, so that the strength of current may be appreciated which had carried this drift in a few weeks so far along the coast and against a northerly wind.

A fine calm day enabled us to make a careful and close examination within pistol-shot of the shores of Wolstenholme Sound, which we followed without seeing either inhabitants or any traces of human beings till we reached the site of the winter quarters of the North Star, which were marked by the grave-stones of the poor fellows who had died during their long winter's night on that inhospitable shore.

At the back of an extraordinary looking rocky hill, called Mount Dundas, was seen the village —if it deserve so dignified a term—of North Omenak. Wishing to examine the huts and native graves, I landed with a party of officers and men, well prepared with pickaxes and shovels, and commenced our not very pleasing operation.

E 2

Each hut and storehouse was closely looked
into, and from some of the graves we turned out
the filthy clothes and household goods of the
natives, so that nothing of importance might
escape our notice, being anxious that nothing
should be left undone that could for ever set at
rest the malignant story of Adam Beck as to
the murder of Sir John Franklin and his crew
at this spot. A large cairn, composed of un-
usually heavy stones, had quickly caught our
eye, and was as quickly pulled down, for we
remembered that Adam Beck had stated that
the bones of the murdered crew were concealed
in a large cairn. Each of our party therefore
watched with intense eagerness the progress of
demolition; nothing was discovered, however,
but a heap of fish and other bones of animals,
which appeared to have been stored here against
a day of want. Base Adam Beck!

The quantity of seal and walrus flesh concealed in their store-huts, and the bundles of winter clothing, found in their underground hovels,
satisfied us that the natives, of whom we saw
no other sign, were away on their summer hunt-

ing excursions, and would return in the winter to
North Omenak. These people, it would seem
like their more fashionable brethren of our more
civilized shores, change their abodes during
summer and winter. In summer they dwell in
seal-skin tents, shifting them frequently to hunt
for food as well for their present wants as
for their stores in winter ; during the nine dark
months of which they huddle themselves together in an underground burrow, where, by
means of an oil lamp, they manage to sustain
sufficient caloric to keep the body from freezing.
Thus these poor creatures exist, happy during
the plenty of summer ; and unless improvidence
or scarcity should assail them, contented during
that severity of winter which drives all other
animals to some milder regions.

Having carefully examined North Omenak, I
determined to complete the search of Wolstenholme Sound, by steaming, as close as possible,
round the remainder of the bay, for which
purpose we returned on board, and the patent
log being set, we were able to run a series of
fair courses in order to certify the dimensions

of the sound. The result was that the distance
from Mount Dundas to the extreme eastern
shore is fourteen miles, which somewhat re-
duces the present outline of the sound. About
twenty miles from the base of the sound, and
lying about one-eighth of a mile off the north
shore, two small islands, unnoticed on the charts,
were seen, and having taken angles and sketches
to secure their positions, we passed on to the
examination of Granville Bay.

Here I was surprised to observe that two
islands placed in the Admiralty chart, as
blocking up the entrance of that bay, were not
to be seen, and again, that some little distance
off the west point of its entrance, three curiously
shaped low islands of trap formation, lying in
a south line of each other, were not mentioned
there. To satisfy myself of their true position,
we made a board in to the mouth of the bay, and
a sketch was taken of them. These three islands,
I named the Three Sister Bees, after the three
industrious young ladies who had supplied me
with the dolls for the Greenland children.

The two islands, before discovered, were

named the Manson Isles, after our ice-master,
who was the first to observe them; and a neighbouring cape was called after Mr. Abernethy,
who was my second in command.

In passing out of Wolstenholme Sound, between Saunders Island and the main, we saw
numerous glaciers, and wherever the eye was
able to wander far inland, it fell upon nothing
but vast sheets of ice. The sound was tolerably clear of ice, but in the bay there were
many small bergs floating; and on the loose
floe pieces were seen great numbers of walrus
and seal, the former allowing us to approach
close enough to have put a harpoon into them,
had we been so prepared, but our shots only
frightened them; the wary seals generally took
alarm before we could get sufficiently near.

I had now been on deck two days and two
nights without sleep, and nature demanding
some rest, I was obliged to discontinue my
observations for a few hours; but having no
person to take my place in that duty, it much
grieved me, thus to lose the chance of securing
sufficient angles to fix the positions of all the

points and islands ; but as I knew that we were approaching more important ground, I determined to fortify myself for the work that was in store.

The morning of the 24th found us off the remarkable rock of Fitzclarence, which is upwards of 350 feet high, and shaped somewhat like a bell, forming an invaluable landmark for the entrance of Booth Sound. That place I had intended examining, but the wind heading as we neared it, we were obliged to commence beating, and shortly the heavy sea which ensued obliged us to bear up, and we steered away with the intention of taking shelter in Granville Bay ; however, when near Blackwood Point, the wind moderated, and under steam we endeavoured to push along the shore in the direction of Cape Parry. Numerous bergs, however, which had grounded off Booth Sound, rendered it difficult to approach, and clearly shewed that shoal water lay off it, and as we neared the northern point of the entrance of the sound, the wind, again freshening and heading, obliged us again to put the helm up, and so we

bore away a second time for Granville Bay. A
third time the same change occurring, I determined to try and beat against it, and at last
succeeded in holding our own, though we passed
a stormy night.

Here the strong northerly set was again detected close in shore, sweeping us up each time
towards the point from which we had run back,
and not unfrequently giving us cause for much
anxiety on account of the grounded bergs, as
we drove so rapidly past, that we had some
difficulty in clearing them.

The gale we had been expecting blew with
some fury, and the ship having been placed
under snug sail with her head off shore, we
roughed it out till noon of the 25th, when we
found ourselves about fifteen miles east of the
Cary Islands. There I obtained a good latitude,
and my sights at nine supplied a tolerable longitude ; these with the variation and true bearings, observed at the same time, proved useful
matter on which to base my new work, as my
friend the Hydrographer, had warned me that
all land to the northward of the Cary Islands

was new, and so in earnest I commenced a careful running survey.

The fine clear sunny day that now smiled upon us, having enabled us to pass Cape Parry within a mile and a half, we closely inspected the shore, and soundings were obtained at forty-five fathoms,—light coloured sand. A small bight, two miles by patent log inside the cape, was passed, and soundings obtained there of the same depth. Cursorily examining this little bight, I should consider a vessel might find tolerable anchorage, and on a pinch, perhaps, conceive a winter harbour might be secured there, as a low reef seems to protect its entrance.

Passing on, we came upon a stream of fresh water-ice, and being now rather short of water, having pumped out our tanks rather too soon, we got on board, in ballast baskets, a quantity of the purest ice, which, though floating in the briny element, when melted has no brackish taste, and is generally found purer than the melted snow.

Dr. Sutherland was actively employed in collecting sea-weed, which we found floating in great abundance. Some pieces that he obtained, when examined, proved to be encrusted with *zoophytes* and *serpulæ*, and the roots to contain bivalve and other varieties of shell.

The sea literally swarmed with forms of the most minute dimensions :—The *cetochilus*, widely distributed here, attains an unusual size, one or two of these which we obtained were three quarters of an inch in length, and of the *sagitta* some were fully two inches long :—*beroe* are most abundant, and the *clio* and *limacine* meet the eye in every cubic foot of water :—Specimens of all these were preserved by our excellent naturalist, who worked with untiring zeal in this branch of research.

After running twenty-one miles from Cape Parry along the shore, huts were observed in a bight that proved to be a small deep water bay, and shortly afterwards natives were observed running about, and evidently anxious that we should approach the shore.

When near enough, the boat was lowered and the doctor, Mr. Abernethy, and myself landed, to make some acquaintance with the new comers.

The same fear was observed as at Petowak ; and the same means having tranquillized them, we soon established ourselves on a friendly footing with them.

They at first indulged in the most extravagant laughter and gesticulation, examining our clothing and our boat with unfeigned wonder and admiration ; they were swathed in furs and skins, and as filthy as can well be imagined; no kyacks were seen, though numerous dogs and sledges were found at their summer habitations, which I lost no time in visiting, as, having no interpreter, it was by this means I hoped to learn intelligence of our missing countrymen.

Their miserable winter hovels were passed on our way to their summer tents, and one of the former having the door blocked up by a stone, which I removed, was found to contain the dead body of a man. I have since learnt that it is a frequent custom with Esquimaux, when the last of a family dies to let his house form his tomb, and leaving him where he died, close up the aperture, and forsake the neighbourhood.

After walking for about a mile and a half we

came to the summer tents, which were miserably dirty and so small that the number intended to dwell in each could only be provided with shelter by huddling together in a mass, with barely room to move hand or foot.

Each hut was carefully searched for European articles of manufacture; but all that could be discovered was a knife-blade, stamped *B. Wilson, cast steel*, and set into an ivory handle, the remains of a hard worked axe without handle, a dilapidated tin canister, and some small pieces of steel, curiously fixed in one piece of bone, so as to form a continuous blade. A piece of rope was found with an eye spliced in one end; but this had so probably been drifted on shore from a whaler, that no importance was attached to it, while the other articles had most probably been obtained in barter with other Esquimaux who had seen whalers further south, and whose well-known nomadic habits might account for their reaching so high a latitude, as within twelve and a half degrees of the pole.

On our way to those summer habitations several stores of blubber and seal and walrus flesh were passed, and round those spots and in the neighbourhood of the dwellings vegetation was quite luxuriant, owing to the accumulation of decomposed animal matter which time had collected.

In some parts rich plots of the *Alopecurus alpinus* and other grasses might indeed have been mowed. The *Cerastium alpinum* and a larged sized *cochlearia* were also abundant. A plant resembling the *Leontodon* evidently a *Taraxacum*, the yellow poppy, the sorrel, *potentillas*, and *saxifrages*, together with *carias*, grew rather profusely along the path towards the summer habitations.

I obtained a stone pot from the natives in exchange for some files, spears, knives, &c. This is a curious work of art and industry; many months were spent in its formation, as it was hewn out of the solid stone, by tools of flint, and hollowed with an exactitude and care that was quite worthy of a civilized hand.

In returning to the boat I ascended an eminence of nearly 1,000 feet in height, and was much struck by observing that what we had

hitherto considered a continuous coast line, was
composed of a group of islands, and that there
seemed to be convenient passages between
them. I lost no time now as it was near midnight in proceeding to the vessel, and finding
her some distance from where I left her, had a
longish sail before I got on board, when I learnt
that she had twice struck rather heavily on a
sunken rock in the middle of the little bay we
had entered. Though she was said to have
trembled fore and aft from the violent concus-
sion, yet I believe no injury was sustained.

In passing between the newly discovered
islands, which I named after his Grace the First
Lord of the Admiralty, Northumberland Island,
and another I called after Sir Thomas Herbert, I
took numerous angles and sketches, but what was
my surprise when I beheld two wide openings to
the eastward, into a clear and unencumbered
sea, with a distinct and unbroken horizon, which,
beautifully defined by the rays of the rising sun,
showed no sign of land save one island, which I
called after that indefatigable Naval Lord of the
Admiralty, Captain Milne.

Another island between it and Herbert
Island, I called after the Earl of Tyrconnel.

This fair strait, which I called after my kind
friend the President of the Royal Geographic
Society, Sir Roderick Murchison, opened out
to us a field for discovery, that proved almost
too tempting for me to withstand the pursuit.
I had a severe struggle in my own mind, but a
sense of duty to our lost countrymen, which
plainly pointed to the northward and westward,
prevailed, and sailing away we manfully turned
our backs on a fairer opportunity for research
and discovery than often falls to the lot of man
to be offered.

On we stood northward, every few miles
making numerous observations and sketches, to
which the well-stocked angle and sketch-book
will bear ample witness. A reef, existing off the
north-west point of Northumberland Island, was
detected by the fleet of icebergs that were
grounded on it. Hakluyt Island, of Baffin, so
incorrectly laid down in the charts, was properly
fixed, and proved to be many miles to the eastward of its supposed position.

The strong northerly set before experienced was still felt, and in a calm off the north point of Northumberland Island, nearly occasioned our falling on board a large grounded berg ; for the current seemed here to be split by the south angle of Prudhoe Island, and thus to set through Murchison Strait as well as towards Smith Sound. Steam got up, we made rapid progress from such an unwelcome associate ; and now, the vessel under full command of steam, sail, and current, we sped away to the northward, and by twelve, P.M., of the 26th, found ourselves within half-a-mile of Cape Alexander, of which the view given may form a tolerable notion. Sounding at this distance from the shore we obtained 145 fathoms—sand and black spots.

We were entering the Polar Sea, and wild thoughts of getting to the Pole—of finding our way to Behring Strait—and most of all, of reaching Franklin and giving him help, rushed rapidly through my brain. A few hours and we should either be secure in our winter quarters, or else plying onward in the unfreezing Polar Basin.

F

CHAPTER IV.

As may well be imagined my time was now
fully engaged, and my pencil and sextant were
rarely out of my hand by night more than by
day. Sea-weed was observed floating in abundance on the water, its roots containing several
species of *asterias* and bivalves, and the sides of
Cape Alexander were covered with bright green
mosses and grasses. This headland is rather
remarkable, and a small island, a little to the
southward, which I called Sutherland Island,
not less so. The shore between Cape Alexander
and Cape Robertson is of that peculiar tabulated
form so remarkable in Lancaster Sound; but this
table-land was broken up by vast glaciers, which
bursting forth through the yielding ravines pour
their yearly tribute of icebergs out upon the deep.

On rounding Cape Alexander the full glory of being actually in the Polar Sea burst upon my thoughts, for then I beheld the open sea stretching through seven points of the compass, and apparently unencumbered with ice though bounded on east and west by two distinct headlands ; the one on the western shore was named after His Royal Highness Prince Albert, as, by a happy coincidence, it was at twelve P.M., on his birthday, that the point was first observed. Immediately to the northward of Cape Alexander some extraordinary table-topped cliffs attracted our notice, and so perfectly even and marked into galleries did they appear, that my mind immediately associating them with the glassy sides of the Great Exhibition, I named them the Crystal Palace Cliffs.

Very careful sketches were made of the headlands, and angles were taken to fix their position.

The changed appearance of the land to the northward of Cape Alexander was very remarkable south of this cape.; nothing but snow-capped hills and cliffs met the eye, but to the northward, an agreeable change seemed to

have been worked by some invisible agency—
here the rocks appeared of their natural black or
reddish brown colour, and the snow, which had
clad with heavy flakes the more southern shore,
had only partially dappled them in this higher
latitude, whilst the western shore, which was
girt with a belt of ice upwards of twelve miles
broad, seemed clad with perpetual snows.

We pushed on while the weather was fair, and
beautiful indeed was the prospect before us ; the
sun had just sheltered himself for an hour
below the horizon, and still shot his rays far
into the northern sky, tinging the snows on the
western land with crimson hues, and throwing
a glow over nature which ill accorded with the
biting cold. As the morning of the 27th
dawned, the wind drew to the northward, and
freshened too much to admit of our steaming—
accordingly the tacks were hauled on board, and
we commenced plying to windward amongst the
bergs and floe pieces, which were now drifting
southward. No time was lost, and every one
on board seemed anxious to push on, but Providence had ordered otherwise, the breeze which

had now increased to a moderate gale, beat sorely against our little barque. Stretching over to the west shore, with a view to making careful search for cairns, we were stopped by the vast body of ice, which was twelve miles in breadth, and firmly fixed to the land. At nine I obtained tolerable sights, but the refraction and encumbered horizon made us far from certain as to the actual altitude of the sun.

As we ran back to the east shore, I measured by patent log the distance, and estimating the ice to be twelve miles wide, I found this part of the entrance to the Polar Basin, thirty-six miles across.

The western land showed at some distance back a high range of mountains, which were called after His Royal Highness the Prince of Wales; and these terminating in the extreme northernmost point that we could see, I called after our most gracious queen, Victoria Head; and the bay intervening between that and Cape Albert, was named after the Princess Marie, present Duchess of Hamilton. Other capes on the west shore were called after the Earl of

Camperdown, Colonel Sabine, Miss Cracroft (niece of Sir John Franklin), and Major Wade. Two high mountains near Cape Isabella were named Mounts Leeds, after His Grace the Duke of Leeds, and my Lord Bolton.

On the eastern land, the furthest northern point we observed, was called after His Danish Majesty King Frederick VII., being the most northern point of his dominions, and in gratitude for the assistance and attention so unreservedly shewn to me by his Majesty's officials at the Greenland settlements.

The nearest bay to this point was called after Lady Franklin, and the next cape south, after my very kind friend, Lord Douglas, now Duke of Hamilton.

Names were given to other points and bays after Admiral Hyde Parker, my friends Mr. Thelluson and Mr. Thorold, and two points to the northward of a cape, which I called after my friend, Lord Hatherton, were respectively named Stafford Head and Pelham Point.

An island just to the northward of the Crystal Palace Cliffs was called Littleton Island, after

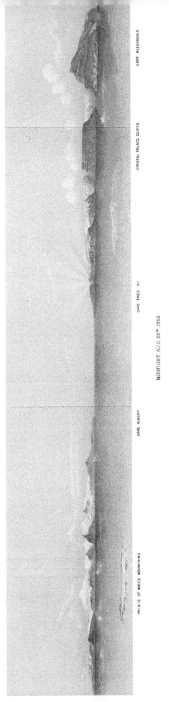

PRINCE OF WALES MOUNTAINS   CAPE ALBERT   CAPE FRED. VII   CRYSTAL PALACE CLIFFS   CAPE ALEXANDER

MIDNIGHT AUG 26ᵀᴴ 1852

The material originally positioned here is too large for reproduction in this reissue. A PDF can be downloaded from the web address given on page iv of this book, by clicking on 'Resources Available'.

the Hon. Mr. Littleton, and afterwards a flat topped isle, seen far north, received the name of Louis Napoleon Island, in honour of the French President, from whom I had received some very flattering attentions.

We continued beating to windward till noon, but now much ice commenced drifting south, and considerably impeded our progress; ice too, was seen far ahead, and by some, an ice-blink was observed to the extreme north, though my own impression is, that there was nothing on the east shore that would have prevented our steaming through, as we did off Cape York. Be that as it may, the wind continued to freshen so rapidly, that we were soon forced to shorten sail, but fortunately clearing up towards noon, I was enabled to get a good observation, from which the altitude being 21° 15′, the latitude of this, our most northerly position, was computed to be 78° 28′ 21″ north, and therefore placing the Isabel about 140 miles further than had been reached by any previous navigator, of whom we have any records. Though the wind had now freshened to a gale, I determined to

hold on our course as long as possible, and
after the people had dined, to seek a landing place. The heavy sea, however, which had
now got up, occasioned by the wind setting
against the strong north current, entirely precluded this, and thus prevented my visiting the
shores of Prudhoe Land, which I called that
country north of Whale Sound, or obtaining
specimens of the rock, or of making some
observations on the needle, or erecting a cairn,
with a notice that the British Flag had been
the first carried into this unknown sea.

It was deemed by every one on board mad-
ness to attempt a landing, and thus I was forced
to relinquish those desires ere we bore up, which
with the heavy gale that now blew, was the
most prudent step I could take. The rest of
the 27th and the following day were spent in
reaching under snug sail on either tack, whilst
the pitiless northerly gale drove the sleet and
snow into our faces, and rendered it painful
work to watch for the icebergs, that we were
continually passing. On this account I could
not heave the ship to, as the difficulty of dis-

cerning objects rendered it imperative that she
should be kept continually under full command
of the helm. The temperature 25°, and the
continual freezing of the spray, as it broke
over the vessel, combined with the slippery
state of the decks from the sleet that fell, and
the ice which formed from the salt water, made
all working of ropes and sails not only dis-
agreeable, but almost impracticable, so that I
was not sorry when the wind moderated.

By four A.M. of the 29th, it fell almost to a
calm, but a heavy swell, the thick fog and
mist remaining, precluded our seeing any distance before us, and thus we imperceptibly drew
too near the land pack off the western shore,
so that a little after Mr. Abernethy had come
on deck in the morning watch, I was called
up, as he said that the ship was drifting rapidly
into the ice. Soon on deck, I found that there
was no question on that score, for even now the
loose pieces were all round us, and the swell was
rapidly lifting the ship farther in to the pack,
whilst the roar of the waters surging on the vast
floe pieces gave us no very pleasant idea of what

would be our fate, if we were fairly entrapped
in this frightful chaos. The whale-boat was
lowered, and a feeble effort made to get her
head off shore, but still in we went, plunging
and surging amongst the crushing masses.

While I was anxiously watching the screw,
upon which all our hopes were now centred, I
ordered the boiler which had been under repair,
and was partly disconnected, to be rapidly
secured, the fires to be lighted, and to get up the
steam ; in the mean time the tackles were got up
for hoisting out our long-boat, and every preparation was made for the worst. Each man on
board knew he was working for his life, and
each toiled with his utmost might ; ice-anchors
were laid out, and hawsers got upon either bow
and quarter, to keep the ship from driving farther in, but two hours must elapse before we
could expect the use of the engine. Eager were
the inquiries when *will* the steam be up ? and
wood and blubber were heaped in the furnace to
get up the greatest heat we could command.

At last the engineer reported all was ready,
and then warping the ship's head round to sea-

DANGEROUS POSITION OF THE "ISABEL" CAUGHT IN THE LEE PACK

ward, we screwed ahead with great caution, and
at last found ourselves, through God's providence and mercy, relieved from our difficulties.

It was a time of the deepest suspense to me ;
the lives of my men and the success of our
expedition, depended entirely on the safety of
the screw, and thus I watched with intense
anxiety the pieces of ice as we drifted slowly past
them ; and, passing the word to the engineer,
"Ease her," "Stop her," till the huge masses
dropped into the wake, we succeeded with much
difficulty in saving the screw from any serious
damage, though the edges of the fan were bur-
nished bright from abrasion against the ice.

I feel sure there was not a heart amongst us
that was not lifted up in gratitude to its Maker,
when we met together for our usual divine
service, and a special thanksgiving was offered
for our marvellous escape from the horrors of a
winter in the pack, or perhaps from wreck among
these frightful masses.

The western shore was now attentively followed with our glasses, and certain capes, inlets,
and bays, named as we passed them, though we

were too far off to do more than take sketches and obtain some angles and bearings.

As soon as the boiler had cooled sufficiently (though it was Sunday night), the engineer and blacksmith recommenced its repairs, and before morning it was finished.

The 30th found us off the headland, which had been called by previous voyagers Clarence Head. Two inlets, seen distinctly to the northward of this, were called after the Earls Talbot and Cadogan, and a series of points were named Gale Point, Paget Point, Dunsterville Head, Cape Faraday, Bence Point, Boger Point, and Cape Combermere, the latter after the Viscount Combermere.

A small island to the northward of this point was called after the daughter of one of my friends, Mittie Island, and a double coned mountain, a little to the northward of Clarence Head, named Mount Glentworth, after the Dowager Viscountess Glentworth. On the 31st, at four A.M., we entered Glacier Strait, and though under steam, and though it was nearly calm, little progress was made, not moving

much more than three knots, owing to the set
out of Jones' Sound, which I consider was at
the rate of almost two miles an hour to the
eastward ; various observations, angles, and
sketches, were taken to fix Cobourg and Kent
Islands, and the several headlands.

Light variable winds springing up towards
noon, we commenced plying to windward, but
closely examining the coast as we passed along,
not a rock or stone, that did not receive from
one of the many telescopes always ready, the
closest scrutiny.

We were not unfrequently startled by rocks
that had the appearance of cairns, and crevices
in the glacier that were mistaken for flagstaffs,
and sometimes by the singular appearance of
smoke seen amongst the hills, and well known to
Arctic voyagers, as a kind of steam or fog that
is drawn from certain parts, by what I suppose to
be unequal radiation.   The night of the 31st
was spent in beating against the westerly wind,
which had now freshened to a stiff breeze, and
Cone Island and Smith Island were passed.
A cape on the north shore of Glacier Strait

was called C. Tennyson, in honour of the Poet
Laureat, and an extraordinary shaped island,
reached about noon of the 1st September, was
called Sir Robert Inglis Peak.   Indifferent
observations only could be obtained, for the
drifting ice so encumbered the sea, it was almost
impossible to be sure of the horizon, and here
and there it was obstructed by vast icebergs,
150 feet in height.

The time was now approaching when we
must expect to be frozen in, and I began to
cast about an anxious eye, for a winter harbour; nothing however that could afford a
shelter from the rigours of a northern winter
could be observed, and it was also evident that
we must not long remain in our present position,
unless sheltered by some land that would give
protection from the drift ice.

Already we had passed through vast fields of
floe pieces, some of them five and twenty feet in
thickness, and a change of wind would bring
them back upon us with a crushing violence that
nothing could withstand; still on we plied, till
after our observations at noon, made just to the

southward of Inglis Peak, when to our surprise,
on drawing a little farther to the westward,
we found the north shore suddenly turning
away to the northward while the south shore
of the sound continued to stretch away in a
westerly direction, till lost in the distance.
Farther to the westward no land could be discerned, nor was any visible between the extreme
north-west point, and the south shore.

Heavy drifting ice, indeed, was seen everywhere, and we had already found much difficulty in plying through what we had passed in
the forenoon.

It was foggy at two o'clock, and, therefore,
little could be done in the way of examining
the shore, and feeling the responsibility of
remaining in such a dangerous position, at this
late season of the year, I felt it my duty to
determine at once, upon quitting a locality,
which, from the fog, we had no opportunity
of examining; where the shores presented so
bold and rugged a front, that no human foot
could have found a resting place; and neither
anchorage, nor shelter of any sort, could be

obtained. Accordingly, having attained the longitude of 84° 10' W., in the latitude of 76° 11' N., we bore up, and running over to the south shore, before the gale, which had commenced to blow with some violence, we examined, in the intervals of fog, every rock with our glasses, naming certain headlands as we passed, after my very kind friend Mr. Macdonald, the Master Attendant of Woolwich Dockyard (to whom I felt so much indebted for his valuable aid), Mr. Newman Smith, and my old mess-mate and chum, Lieut. Hardy.

The extreme points discovered on the north shore were called Cape Eden, after the kind and excellent Commodore at Woolwich Dockyard, Cape Waldegrave, in honour of the Earl of that name, and Cape Maxwell, after Sir William Maxwell, my good friend of Calderwood Castle.

Rapidly we sped before the freshening gale, towards the eastward, and eagerly did our glasses scan the shore, but it was all in vain, no trace of anything human could we observe, all was a mass of ice. The southern land differs somewhat from the northern in general aspect, the latter being broken up by glaciers, while the former presents a more uniform outline of snow-clad mountains and hills, with their black bases, fringed with sea-washed rock, and projecting into the sound.

Before such a gale as we now experienced, we were not long in passing through Lady Anne's Strait, but little did we anticipate the danger which awaited us.

The wind falling light towards the morning of the 2nd, in a fog, we suddenly found ourselves under the cliffs of Cape Parker, and surrounded by heavy floe ice on every side. The beetling cliffs rose in solemn grandeur over our mast heads, whilst ice, thick heavy ice, hemmed in our little vessel. A gale, or even a stiff breeze from either east or north, would have cast us a miserable wreck on this iron-bound coast, or crumpled her up like an empty eggshell—but we were again spared,—and after some hours of the greatest exertion and wearing anxiety, we found a lane open, which admitted of our steaming out of all these difficulties.

Thankful, most thankful, did we all feel for

G

this liberation from one of two great disasters, which appeared to be our inevitable fate—a winter in the pack, or shipwreck on Cape Parker; but we were still mercifully and harmlessly carried on through all our many perils.

Having steamed out to an offing, it was necessary now to decide what should be our next step; and after much deliberation, I determined to risk the chance of being caught, by freezing-up, and of spending the winter out here, for the benefit that I might confer upon the service in which we were mutually engaged, by carrying my surplus provisions, stores, and coals to the squadron of Sir Edward Belcher, and by giving him an account of my discoveries, as well as the latest intelligence from England, only seven weeks old. In that case, too, I might carry back to England, which there was no doubt that I could reach before the winter, the latest intelligence of the movements of the squadron, and of their chances of success.

I thought the benefit to the country, and the satisfaction to the friends of the missing and searching navigators, would be well worth

the risk and exertion, I therefore determined
upon making an effort to reach the shores of
Beechey Island, where I knew the depôt ship
North Star, was lying.

Light variable winds prevented our effecting
that object before the 7th September, when it
produced no little surprise as the Isabel was
seen steaming round the point of Erebus and
Terror Bay.

When we were near enough to see from our
crow's-nest the mast heads of the North Star, I
had ordered one of the twelve pounders to be
fired, and the people who were working on shore
were greatly puzzled at hearing such a sound, as
they believed that nothing human but their
own party could be within hundreds of miles of
them.

The temperature had now become sufficiently
cold to freeze the seas as they broke over our
vessel, the consequence was that our bows were
one mass of ice, and the anchor, which had
been frozen to the vessel's side, required a considerable degree of coaxing to get it adrift;
by the time, however, we reached a good berth

on the port bow of the depôt ship, all was ready, and we came too in fourteen fathoms water.

There was a good deal of loose drifting ice on the outside of the bay, and young ice was forming very rapidly in the still water near the shore. I soon waited upon Captain Pullen, who kindly had sent a boat to render any assistance we might require, and giving him the letters and papers I had brought from England for the squadron, received in return all the intelligence relative to the search, and hearty congratulations on what we had ourselves done towards that great object.

The North Star had been in some peril since the departure of the squadron, by the breaking up of the ice in the bay, which was of last year's formation, and into which they had with much labour cut their way to an anchorage. A gale of wind had caused it to break up suddenly, and the ship was well nigh drifted out into the strait by the vast masses that accumulated round her bows.

Sir Edward Belcher and Captain Kellett had sailed from Beechey Island, with their steam-

tenders, about three weeks previously, the former up Wellington Channel and the latter to
Melville Island; nothing since had been heard
of either of them, and it was supposed that Sir
Edward had gone away into open water, beyond
Parry Strait. Dr. Macormick had left the
North Star in a boat for the purpose of examining Prince Alfred and Baring Bays, and had
at the time we arrived been absent a fortnight.

One of the officers, who by his disappointed
face I could see had received no letter, offered
to take me on shore, and shew me the relics
of the missing squadron, while the others were
preparing their despatches; for we could only
afford to give them a few hours, wishing to be off
on our own search, and fearing that delay might
oblige us to winter in that strait, to which we did
not feel at all inclined, after our disappointment
in securing winter quarters to the northward.

That sad emblem of mortality—the grave
—soon met my eye, as we plunged along
through the knee-deep snow which covered the
island. The last resting place of three of
Franklin's people was closely examined; but

nothing that had not hitherto been observed could we detect. My companion told me that a huge bear was seen continually sitting on one of the graves keeping a silent vigil over the dead.

Having picked up some of the meat canisters with which the island is strewed, and made a collection of some of the relics of canvas and wood which were still found scattered here and there, we returned towards the boat, and were shown the wooden house that the North Star's crew were building for the reception of a party of sixty people, should occasion require it. This house, which was of large dimensions, was being made of the wood collected in Melville Bay from the wrecks of the two ships that had been crushed there this year, and was to be called Sion House, after the residence of the Duke of Northumberland.

The Mary yacht, left out by Sir John Ross, was seen lying on the beach, and not the worse for the rigours of the climate.

On my return to the North Star, the excitement of letter reading and writing having somewhat abated, I went to the commander's cabin,

there to obtain the latest information of the
Belcher squadron.

Sir Edward's views, prospects, and chances
of success, were all fully discussed, and I learnt
with no small pleasure that the season I had
found so open was apparently the same in this
neighbourhood.   It was the intention of Captain
Pullen to effect a communication by sledges
with Sir Edward in the spring of the ensuing
year, and a rendezvous had been fixed between
them for such a meeting.   I pressed upon
Captain Pullen the acceptance of all my surplus
stores and provisions, and such a proportion of
my coal as I could spare, but, prohibited by his
commanding officer from in any way to inter-
fere with any private vessel, he declined all
the offers I made, and I did not choose to risk
the loss of the stores by landing them on
Beechey Island, as Mr. Kennedy had done.

Dr. Sutherland and myself dined with the
Captain and Officers, and we were regaled with
luxuries and delicacies of we knew nothing in
the Isabel.   Soft bread, *loon* pie, beer, and other
niceties, composed part of the meal.

Learning indirectly of what stores the officers' mess were shortest, I sent them a hundred weight of potatoes, and the same quantity of preserved beef and ox cheek, as a present from Lady Franklin, which was gratefully accepted ; but I could not induce them to accept anything for the public service, though I offered all as a free gift, now that I was likely to return this season, and being anxious to carry out Lady Franklin's original intention.

It was midnight ere the letter bags were pre-pared and all the kind farewells said, but the steam being up, and a light wind favouring, and anxious to lose no time unnecessarily, we tripped the anchor and shortly after twelve pushed out of the bay, with as beautiful a moon to light our path as ever shone on the favoured shores of our own native land.

The following day the wind headed and freshened as we pressed on towards the east-ward, anxious to escape from the grasp of the winter, which was now following us with rapid strides from the icy north. A day or two of buffeting against this foul wind ran our water

very low, and I once feared we should have to
put back to Beechey Island for that necessary
article, the snow we had collected there being
all consumed. A tank, however, was found in
the main hold which had not been broached, and
thus we were enabled to prolong our struggle,
and by the 12th we were well off Mount
Possession.

Here we experienced a curious instance of
the difficulties which assail the mariner in these
seas. Beating against a southerly wind at
dusk, a thick fog came on, and thus obscured
the land from which we were not far off. The
compass being here perfectly useless, and the
moon and stars being absent, we continued to
thrash to windward the whole night, at the
end of which I was not a little chagrined, on
seeing the direction of the sun, to find that—
we could not tell how long—we had been
beating against a fair wind, which had come
round during the hours of mist and darkness.
I never so fully appreciated the meaning of my
family motto, "The sun, my compass." Pro-

vidential indeed was it that we had not thus been
led into some more serious difficulty. The helm
was soon put up, and away we went before the
favouring gale, searching with eager gaze the
western shore, as we ran down the coast, and as
near as was considered prudent. At night we
fired guns and threw up rockets to attract the
attention of any poor wanderers that might be
looking for succour.

On the 14th we were off Cape Bowen, and I
landed to look for traces and erect a cairn;
nothing, however, could be seen but the bold
footprint of a huge bear and the tiny track of a
small arctic fox. I observed the dip here, but
the cold driving sleet prevented my taking the
proper series of observations for the variation.

A cairn was erected to mark the spot of our
visit, and some specimens of the rock collected
for my kind friend Sir Roderick Murchison.
We then returned on board, and shaping our
course along the land continued our examination
as far as Cape Adair, where I again attempted
to land, but the brash ice extending a mile off

the shore quite prevented it, and thus, after
losing much time, we returned on board to
continue our course, which lucklessly was soon
stopped by a body of ice with which we fell in
off Scott Inlet, firmly packed on to the shore.

CHAPTER V.

HAVING failed in landing at Cape Adair we were obliged to content ourselves with scraping up anything with our dredge in the depth of twenty fathoms. The bottom we found composed of decayed rock forming a fine sand, which I think would be tolerable holding-ground, and as there does not seem to be more than twenty-six fathoms at two miles' distance, a ship might safely anchor there for a tide, if the ice was not too near a neighbour.

When fully assured of the impossibility of getting farther along the coast, I determined to press along the edge of the pack and seek for an opening to carry us again in shore that our search might be continued, and on the 16th I fancied we were about to effect this desirable

object, but to my distress I found we were running into a deep bight, out of which it afterwards cost us some hours to work. The ice that
seems to have been collected at this point by the
great bergs which had grounded on the Hecla
and Griper Banks, had doubtless been drifted
out of the northern sounds, and carried south by
the continual set in that direction experienced
on these western shores.

My ice-masters informed me that not unfrequently the whalers are thus prevented from
coasting to the southward from Pond Bay, but
that when the ice hangs about the River Clyde
(which lies a little to the southward of Scott
Inlet) they are usually obliged to stretch over
to Disko before they can get away south.
However, on the morning of the 17th, I was
in great hope that we were to be rescued from
our difficulties, for a strong breeze accompanied
by a heavy sea from the south-eastward gave us
cause to think that there was clear water far to
windward, and that we had really rounded the
tail of the ice.

On the 18th, hoping now to make a little

southing, with the view of getting in with the
west coast, we stood away in that direction, but
were not a little mortified at observing the pack
stretching right across our bows and not very far
ahead.   Again we stretched to the northward,
and on the 19th, hoping we had got far enough
to the eastward, another attempt was made to
close the west shore, and steam was got up, the
wind falling light.   Towards noon a gentle
breeze springing up, we were enabled to dis-
pense with the use of our engine, and as it was
Sunday I was glad to be able to give the smutty
stokers their day of rest.   Thick snow fell in
heavy flakes during the afternoon, and beating
down the wind, soon left us lying with all sail
set, flapping lazily to and fro, and waiting for
the breeze to freshen, which the state of the
barometer gave us every reason to expect.   Sitting reading in my cabin about five o'clock, I
was startled by feeling the vessel suddenly heel
over, and great was my surprise on reaching
the deck to find that a squall had suddenly
struck us, and split several of the sails, and
carried away many sheets and haulyards, while

the flapping of the torn wet canvas made it both difficult to hear the word of command to shorten sail, and still more difficult to do what was ordered. Our "Big Tom" was split to ribbons in the head, but this I soon found was rather hailed with delight by Jack, for as it was a spare mainsail, fitted to set between the foremast and mainmast, it was not very handy to manage, and though useful in light winds had not won good opinions from those who had to furl or set it.

Ere a quarter of an hour, the sea which had been before so smooth now became so rough and boisterous, as to break clean over all. Each plunge loading the rigging and spars with long milk-white icicles, and stiffening by freezing everything it fell upon.

None but those who have voyaged in these seas, and taken a share in the manual labour of working the vessel as I have done, can know the discomfort of labour under such difficulties, each rope, each sail, to be handled, are as though they were made of oak instead of hemp, and freeze to the flesh if touched by the bare hand.

The rest of Sunday and the following day were spent in beating against the strong north gale which followed the squall.

The pack we knew was not far under our lee, and thus we were compelled to make every effort to keep it there; but on the 21st, the weather moderating, we made an attempt to get *through* it, and accordingly dashed boldly into the middle of the pack. Pancake ice was forming rapidly everywhere, warning us that delay would be dangerous, and I am now convinced, had we not been supplied with steam-power, we should in a few hours have been sealed up for the winter.

We struggled on with our ice-masters in the crow's-nest, conning the ship into the lanes of open water as they seemed to invite in the direction we wished to go. About four o'clock in the afternoon, while busy in my cabin at my charts, I was informed that three bears were near us on the ice, and our poor dogs really needing a fresh meal (having supplied Captain Pullen with the remainder of my Cape York bears), I eagerly set off in pursuit of the intruders. The trio were evidently composed of a mother

and twins; and being rather anxious to secure
the latter, for carrying to England alive, I fired
cautiously at the mother, but not being successful
in hitting her the first time in a vital spot, I
was obliged, as she scampered over the ice, to
fire such random shots, that I wounded one and
killed the other of her cubs, and it was nearly
seven o'clock before all three were secured, and
hoisted on board. Poor Mrs. Bruin! it was quite
heart rending to see the affection that existed
between her and her cubs. The latter when
they saw their mother wounded, regardless of
their own sufferings, commenced licking her
wounds, whilst she with that natural instinct,
observable amongst all wild animals, scraped
snow up with her huge paw and plastered it
upon the bleeding part, to staunch the blood by
its styptic effects.

When she began to eat the snow we knew
she was mortally wounded, but even then her
care for the cubs did not cease, as she kept continually turning her head from one to the other,
and, though roaring with pain, she seemed to
warn them to escape if possible; but their attach-

H

ment was as great as hers, and thus I was obliged to destroy them all. It went much against my feelings, but the memory of my starving dogs reconciled me to the necessity.

Three hours spent thus brought night so close upon us, that we were obliged to seek about for a large berg to which we might moor the vessel till morning; and shortly finding one, sail was shortened and our hawsers secured to it.

A calm lovely night, with brilliant Aurora and star-lit sky, gave symptoms of fine weather, which in our present position was much to be desired, although a little wind would be beneficial to keep the ice sufficiently in motion to prevent our being frozen in; still a gale was much to be dreaded, and I lay down hoping that the morning might see us well through into the east water.

The quiet rest all hands had enjoyed, freshened us for work when morning broke on the 22nd; and at four A.M. steam having been got up, we slipped, and screwed away, with the aid of a light northerly wind, in the direction of a water-blink which our ice-masters spied to the southward.

In two hours we had pushed our way into an open sea, and the wind freshening, the fires were soon banked up, and all sail made.

The noon of the 23rd found us 117 miles south of our position on the previous day, in 69° 41′ N. We did not find the strong southerly set, usually experienced at this time of the year in Davis Strait; indeed by comparing our dead reckoning with the observation it was found that a slight northerly set had affected the distance we had made.

By four P.M., the wind had chopped round to the southward, and we were forced to commence beating with the assistance of steam, however it soon freshened too much for the latter, and we were forced to trust to our canvas, which before night was reduced to storm-sails, a southerly gale having set in with much violence.

It soon became evident that the schooner must be hove to, and accordingly all sail was shortened to fore-trysail and close-reefed mainsail, and thus we lay for the whole of the 24th and four following days in such a gale as I had never before witnessed, and accompanied with the heaviest sea I had ever seen, even off Cape Horn. Great was the discomfort felt by all on board, those living abaft especially, for the extreme heat of the engine-room had so parched the under side of the upper deck, that every sea that tumbled on board drained through the seams as it would through a sieve, which added to the violent motion made us feel doubly miserable.

At this time, too, my own strength seemed to fail, and the want of warm tea and such comforts as to a sick man are essential were denied me; for no fire could be kept alight, and all were obliged, for the most part of the time, to content themselves with cold provisions.

Mountainous seas toppled so continually over us, flooding the decks fore and aft, that it was quite impossible to keep the galley fire alight, for when it could be coaxed into a miserable flame, a torrent of water would put it out and carry the struggling cook into the lee scuppers, there to scramble up his pots and pans which had followed his fortunes from the galley side. Those who talk of the misery of a sea life, when perhaps their experience is limited to a passage across the Channel, or to a voyage in a spacious man-of-war, can form no conception of what we sailors call being miserable, but which I must confess during some eighteen years of a sea life, I had never fairly experienced till now. Right glad was I when this tremendous gale began to break, for though the Isabel behaved nobly, it was not a little dangerous driving amongst icebergs, which the drifting sleet and snow made it hard to distinguish from the foaming crests of the waves.

Everything had to be lashed and doubly lashed, but notwithstanding this, our spare spars got adrift, the boat's falls were chafed through, planks were washed overboard, and heartily did we long for "the calm that comes after the storm."

At last the long expected lull allowed us to look about, and to see the damage we had sustained from the fury of the elements; water being the first thing thought of, we soon found that there was too little on board 'to admit of our remaining more than a few days longer at sea, a great quantity that had been stowed for present use on deck, having been spoilt by the salt water getting into the tanks.

The rigging, too, was so much rubbed, and sails so torn, that I soon found it was not only expedient, but absolutely necessary, that we should put into the nearest port. I had been anxious to reach Holsteinburg, in order to run a meridian distance across to the west shore, but the Whale-fish Islands being the nearest point we could coveniently make, we steered for them, and on the 2nd of October, after a few days of light winds, found ourselves off a small group called the Hunde Islands, a little south of the Whale-fish, and by noon observing the flag-staff on the top of a low hill, which marks the settlement, we steered in, and brought up in seven fathoms of water, amongst a cluster of rocky islands which forms good shelter from any gale. The governor came on board to see what our business was at this late season of the year, but our weather beaten appearance soon told the tale for itself, that stress of weather had forced us in to refit.

The remainder of Saturday was occupied in getting out the long-boat, and making every preparation for work on the Monday morning.

The Sabbath was kept as a day of rest, I allowed the men to go on shore for a walk after divine service, and all seemed monstrously to enjoy the opportunity of stretching their legs. They roamed over the islands, visiting the Esquimaux huts, and collecting curiosities to take to England for their Polls or Sues.

We all thoroughly enjoyed this quiet day after the excitement and anxiety of the past week; for myself, I confess that the rest of mind was most enjoyable, and filled my soul with gratitude to Him, who "maketh the storm a calm, so that the waves thereof are still;" and, indeed, that gladness of which the psalmist speaks when he says—" Then are they glad, because they be quiet; so he bringeth them unto their desired haven ;" seemed to take full possession of one's whole heart.

Monday, the 4th October, was commenced by watering the ship, and a lake on one of the near islands proved most useful for this pur-

pose. I engaged eight or ten Esquimaux, who
readily undertook the work without any terms,
and moreover completed it without supervision
or the slightest trouble.

Having no casks, we were obliged to clear
and clean the long-boat out, and then towing her
to the nearest point of the lake, filled her with
water and brought her alongside, when the
Esquimaux completed the friendly operation of
baling and pumping the water into our tanks.
The 5th and 6th proving calm fine days, I was
enabled to swing the ship for local attraction,
and was much surprised at finding how great
the deviation had become.

An island, fifteen miles distant, seemed a
good object for the constant bearing, and
the islands and rocks surrounding the vessel
proved very useful for securing the hawsers,
which were employed to cast the ship's head
to each point of the compass. In the appendix will be found the result of these obser-
tions, and by a comparison with the second and
fourth columns, it will be seen how much the
local attraction had altered with the difference

of latitude, according to our proximity to the magnetic pole and its rapidly varying dip.

I obtained a good set of observations on shore for latitude and longitude, and the variation, dip, and intensity of the needle.

On the 5th, I received a message from the governor, that as it was the King of Denmark's birthday, the Esquimaux would assemble at his house, and have a dance, and the pleasure of my company was solicited for the occasion; accordingly at six o'clock I repaired to the wooden palace of his Excellency, and there found, crammed into a smallish chamber, as many Esquimaux as could conveniently stand.

I had prepared myself with certain bottles by which punch could be quickly made; and several of the officers and crew joining the party, by their assistance, each of the Esquimaux ladies was first supplied with a glass full of the beverage, and afterward the gentlemen, when I made them understand that they were to give three cheers for the King of Denmark, which was done with a vigour and goodheartedness, that made the wooden walls echo again.

I had prepared another treat for them, which I am quite sure was to many the most agreeable of the two. My coxswain came in to tell me when all was ready, and then I begged the governor would tell the party to go outside, where I had somewhat to shew them.

When all were assembled, the booming of one of our guns, which by signal was fired from the vessel, not a little alarmed some of the most timid, and their fear was not much allayed, when, from under their very noses, a shower of rockets flew into mid-air, with a whirl that startled some of the more ancient sages amongst them, though when no damage was found to accrue to any of the party, the shouts of joy overpowered the noise of the rockets.

The blue lights and white lights, which were burnt to enliven the performance, were objects of great curiosity, and I could see some enquiring faces, eagerly watching our movements, as the port-fires were placed to ignite them.

Dancing was afterwards commenced, and feeling that it was my duty to lead off with the governor's wife, who was an Esquimaux, I

begged the honour of her hand, for a dance, in
the best Esquimaux of which I was master, and
to the scraping of a disabled fiddle, bound round
with twine and splints, I launched into the mysteries of an Esquimaux quadrille, which, but for
the strenuous exertions of my partner, to keep
me right, I should certainly have set into utter
confusion.

It was composed of a *chaine des dames* and
a reel, complex to a wonderful degree, and
exhausting to a frightful extent; and yet it
appeared to be the determination of the whole
party to continue at this one figure till tired
nature sunk.

Unaccustomed to this kind of violent exercise,
I was soon knocked-up, and tried, though un-
successfully, to make my escape; but at last
I had the gratification of observing an elderly
lady opposite beginning to falter, and out of
compliment to her I presume this dance was
terminated.

The Esquimaux seem to think it is impossible
to be too warm, so the doors and windows were
tightly closed, and certain lamps and tallow

candles (with which I had supplied his Excellency,) soon brought the temperature up to blood heat.

After resting from my labour, I determined to try their waltz, which I found was not very unlike ours, being performed somewhat in the same manner, and the fair ladies with whom I now alternately figured instructing me in the mysteries of the measure. Some of my sailors having obtained permission to attend the ball, they were now solicited to give a specimen of their skill, and accordingly a sailor's hornpipe and reel, with the usual heel and toe accompaniment, met with great applause.

I had had sufficient fun by nine o'clock, but the party did not break up till after twelve; before I went away, however, at my special request, some Esquimaux melodies were sung by the party, and afterwards a Danish national hymn by the governor. When the officers and men were returning in their boat to the ship they were serenaded by the ladies of the party, who joining hand-in-hand walked along the rocks towards the ship, singing a plaintive air,

which might well have been taken for their
evening hymn. And such it may have been,
for these poor people, demi-civilized and in-
structed as they have been by the Danes, are
full of fervour and zeal for their religion, the
Lutheran, and show more real moral principle
than any nation I ever visited.

The strictest honesty and the most unflinch-
ing observance of truth appeared to be such
marked features of their character, that among
our Greenland sailors it is quite proverbial;
so that, while on the west coast of Davis Strait
they are notorious thieves, on the eastern shore,
where the blessings of religion and civilization
are somewhat known, nothing can exceed their
honesty.

It was the morning of the 7th ere we were
quite ready for sea; and having sent the
Governor some fuel, candles, and sugar, of
which he stood sorely in need, we were about
to trip anchor, when his Excellency came on
board to express his gratitude for my gift, and
bringing a reindeer skin, begged my acceptance
of it.

I was anxious not to lose the breeze which bid fair for getting out of this little archipelago; so, getting his Excellency away as soon as I politely could, we slipped the hawser laid out astern, and away we went before a stiff breeze from the south-eastward, which however soon freshened to a very troublesome gale from the southward, and before nightfall we were again hove to, buffeting with the elements, though under more comfortable circumstances than the last gale we experienced.

Towards the evening of the 9th the gale broke, and we began to make over in earnest to the west shore, but this brief change only ushered in a still more furious gale from the north-eastward, before which we scudded with a high following sea until we were unable to heave to.

Seldom had I witnessed anything equal to what we now experienced : the roaring breakers sweeping furiously before the gale were barely outstripped by our trembling bark, as she seemed to fly in terror before them ; and occasionally, a lofty one, whose velocity was some-

thing greater than our own—perhaps because its
swelling sides had for a time almost becalmed
our sails—came tumbling on board, washing
the poor helmsman almost overboard, and
drenching the deck fore and aft with a sea that
swashed about, owing to the want of proper
scuppers, until it had leeked through the deck
into the cabin below, much to my continual
discomfort, and to the no small detriment of my
books and charts. I had seen very heavy
weather off Cape Horn, where the South Atlantic and Pacific Oceans blend their waters in
mountainous waves, but in no degree did they
equal the seas we experienced in Davis Strait
on our southward passage.

Towards the morning of the 13th the gale
somewhat moderated, but the heavy sea still
remained to annoy us by surging the vessel to
and fro, the yard arms often under water ; and
now, by my dead reckoning, I found the ship
had run past her port, or rather, the inlet I had
wished to make, and in which I had had some
intention of wintering.

At Hogarth Sound, or in the head of
Cumberland Inlet, I had hoped to complete
my search along the west coast of Baffin Bay
by sledges, and then, during the following
spring, to have completed the survey of Davis
Strait, from Cape Walsingham south, as far as
Newfoundland. However, it was ordered
otherwise :

"L'homme propose mais Dieu dispose."

By our reckoning on the 12th, we thought
we should have sighted the land, but we had
seen no appearance of it, and now it was impossible to get in with the shore, and most
dangerous to make an attempt while the sea
was so boisterous. Now, too, the ice-masters
came to me, and urging the lateness of the
season and the dangerous nature of the coast,
entreated me to relinquish all further attempts
to get in with the shore at such a period of
the season, when few hours of daylight afforded
an opportunity for doing anything, and no
chart existed of the coast we were to explore,

though it was certainly known to be guarded by numberless rocks and shoals.

I *could* not reject the sage counsel of my ancient mariners, and therefore, without at once making up my mind on the subject, I told them I would think of it, mentally determining that if the weather did not moderate in forty hours, or some change take place which I could reasonably hope would give us a chance of reaching a place of safety, I would bear up for England.

No change did take place furnishing me with valid excuse for prolonging my stay in these seas, so we put the helm up for our native shores, and I saw many faces brightening as the order was given, some expressing aloud their satisfaction that the perilous voyage we had made had ended so far successfully, and that nothing but the ordinary dangers of a sailor's life was now before them.

I, too, felt thankful, most thankful, to the Almighty for so ordering our goings that we were able to return this winter without one

I

drawback, one accident or mishap, to mar the satisfaction of a voyage which has been called, by the most distinguished authority that can be quoted (Sir Francis Beaufort), one of the most remarkable voyages upon record.

CHAPTER VI.

WE experienced a continuance of heavy weather
while recrossing the Atlantic ; but as nothing
of any importance took place differing from the
usual occurrences of a sea voyage, I will not
dwell upon this part of my journal, but pass on
to our arrival on our own shores, which we
reached on the 4th of November, anchoring at
Stromness the very day four months from our
quitting Woolwich.

We were received with the greatest kindness,
and I was most hospitably entertained by the
family of Dr. Hamilton, a connection of Dr.
Rae, the distinguished Arctic voyager. We
remained a few days at this anchorage, waiting

for a fair wind to carry us through the Pentland
Frith, and from thence we reached Peterhead
on the 10th, where we remained a few hours
to discharge a part of the crew we had shipped
at that place.   It was on the 10th of July that
we had sailed from there, and the 10th of
November found us steering into the little bay
south of the town, very much to the surprise of
the inhabitants, who would hardly credit our
statement when told of what we had accomplished in so short a time.

A part of our crew being discharged, some
letters landed, and fresh provisions procured,
we left Peterhead in the afternoon for Woolwich,
but stress of weather obliging us to put into the
Frith of Forth, I determined to proceed to
London from Edinburgh, and leave a north sea
pilot to bring the fair Isabel to the Thames.

Heavy easterly gales and continuous bad
weather prevented her reaching Woolwich for
some weeks; at last, however, she safely arrived,
and by the kind permission of the Admiralty, I
was allowed to lay her alongside the dock yard,
where we returned such surplus stores as had

been drawn from that depôt, and commenced otherwise to dismantle our little barque.

And now that our Arctic voyage is ended, let us calmly review what has been done, what information has been acquired relative to the missing expedition, what addition to geography obtained, and how has been solved the long vexed question of the head of Baffin Bay and its opening into the Polar Basin?

First, upon examining the chart which has been carefully compiled from all the data I could collect in my northern push, it will be seen that the coast on the eastern shore was carefully examined as far north as $78°\ 35'$, and that when natives or their habitations were discovered, the most minute inquiries and the most rigid search were prosecuted amongst them.

Whale Sound was not examined to its farthest extremity, for this reason—that as nothing but the most improbable accident could have brought Sir John Franklin to these shores, I could have no excuse but geographic research for extending my cruise amongst the islands discovered there ;

and as I visited the habitations of the natives, and closely examined their dresses, &c., without discovering any thing that could lead to a supposition that Franklin had ever visited that region, it behoved me to leave this most interesting field for future discovery and to push boldly on for a higher latitude.

Smith Sound was reached, and here nothing betrayed the slightest token of the previous presence of a human being, though there were several prominent and easily accessible points which would have afforded him good opportunities for leaving such marks, or erecting such cairns, that must at once have arrested the eye of a passing mariner. We sought in vain for any thing of the kind ; and though continually within half a mile of the coast nothing foreign to those iron-bound shores could be discovered, though an object the size of a man's hat could hardly have escaped our notice—so perfectly clear and continually bright was the weather.

The gale which forced us to relinquish all farther attempt to get to the northward prevented any other search being made, but such as we could prosecute with our glasses from the deck of the vessel; and this was done by each person who possessed a spy-glass, with an anxiety that often kept one or two of us for the whole night from going to bed.

Jones Sound was next examined but with no better success, no mark or cairn could be observed, and bad weather, the lateness of the season, and other difficulties made it necessary to retreat from that gulf before the winter had commenced in real earnest. In short there is every reason to believe that Franklin never attempted either of the two sounds last mentioned, as he would otherwise have certainly left some indication of his presence; and the latter was observed to be of so different a character to those open sounds we had previously explored, that I could not but consider it as nothing more than a gulf having no outlet, except possibly by some small frozen strait into the Polar Sea.

That Jones Sound is an impenetrable gulf, at least in a westerly direction, I argue from the facts, that while Whale Sound, Smith Sound, and Lancaster Sound, were found free, and navigable apparently to any distance, with strong currents setting into them, Jones Sound was observed to be choked with ice, certainly drifting, but of a thickness which proved it to be of many years' formation, and thus unquestionably seldom driven out of that locality.

Icebergs were seen in it as far as 84° W., of vast dimensions, some 150 feet in height, and this may be considered an essential feature differing widely from the other sounds.

The set of the current observed in Jones Sound was to the eastward, but slight, and we had no opportunity of determining whether it was permanent, or, as in other parts of Baffin Bay, wholly dependent on the prevailing winds. That the western extremity of Jones Sound is closed, I have little doubt, but that it may open a way to the northward by a frozen strait, is very possible, for this reason, that the current which was detected in carrying out to the eastward, ice, of many years' formation, must have had some corresponding inlet; and thus the sound, though not altogether a *cul-de-sac* has

such a small and contracted inlet towards the
Polar Sea, as not to allow of the ice escaping,
or indeed to give any impulse to it, excepting
on such occasions as this very favourable summer. To this I may add, that Dr. Sutherland was the person, who in the expedition of the
foregoing year, explored the north-east shore
of Wellington Channel and Penny Strait, and
he feels perfectly assured that a range of mountains intervenes between Baring Bay and the
western head of Jones' Sound.

Lancaster Sound was visited by us from two
motives—one in order to give Sir Edward
Belcher the advantage of our discoveries, and
the other that should I be able to return this
season to England, I could in that case convey
the latest intelligence of the government expedition to those most interested about it; these
objects appeared to me to be forcible enough to
induce me to determine upon going there, and
thus risking the sacrifice of all our own ulterior
intentions to them.

The west coast of Baffin Bay, as far south as
the river Clyde, was examined as well as our

feeble means would admit, but with no better results than the others.

Our object here was to search for the crews of the berg-borne ships, which some supposed might have been wrecked on these shores, or at least that they might have escaped to land as the vessels were driven south on their icy cradles. To give notice of our position, rockets and guns were fired at night, and a boat put in to the shore twice to seek for traces, but none could be found, and with this our search for the missing expedition ended.

Secondly.—With regard to the geographic information obtained, I may again quote the words of the hydrographer of the Admiralty, who in a letter to me says, " Remember from the Cary Islands to the northward all is new, as well as the interior of Jones Sound."

A reference to the chart will show how much has been added from Cape Parry northwards, and besides this addition of 600 miles of continuous new coast line, several alterations and additions were made to the previously imperfect outline with which we were supplied.

The meteorological journal, which has been most carefully and strictly kept, and registered every three hours by my indefatigable friend, Dr. Sutherland, will, I think, prove of some importance by its comparison with that of Sir Edward Belcher's expedition in Wellington Channel. And the fruits of the Doctor's dredge, in the several new species of marine animals; and the sea-weeds, as well as plants, brought to England by him, will be found not uninteresting to those, who, like himself, are devoted to the natural history of these northern climes.

To those persons who understand the value of such research, the examination of the sea-water will suggest ideas with reference to the whale fisheries that may be worth more than the passing consideration—especially now that our fisheries are so rapidly declining.

In Whale Sound, the two well known forms of molusca, called the *clio borealis* and *sagitta,* were observed to be larger and in greater quantity than elsewhere; and I cannot but feel persuaded that a season spent in waters where the whale's food is found in such abundance must prove a fruitful field for the exertions of the industrious whaler. Several whales were seen by our people while there, and the natives shewed us some of the vertebræ evidently obtained from the carcase of a dead fish which had been thrown ashore, as they had no kyacks or means of capturing the live animal.

Whale Sound, opening as it did upon our view, with several large islands and fine inlets, affords a scope for future search, which I think from the singular similarity that it possesses to its opposite neighbour Lancaster Sound, as there we neither saw ice nor bergs, would well repay the adventurous whaler, or the discovery ship, by its examination.

On the whole, I think it not improbable that the land intervening between Lancaster and Smith Sounds, as well as that on the east shore between Whale Sound and the latter, will one day prove to be a group of islands, though now ranging themselves apparently into continuous coast-lines, which form the limits of Baffin Bay.

These islands, I have every reason to believe,
are only the portals, if I may use such a term,
of the great Polar Basin; aud if penetrated
with prudence and in a fair season, will perhaps
effect a readier communication with the missing
expedition, and earlier solve the north-west passage problem, than pursuing our comrades in
their own footsteps, on the route which, we
think, they must have followed.

For myself, I wish no better fortune than to
be allowed next year to follow up the discoveries
we have made, and should I be lucky enough
to reach these new shores, at the beginning, instead of at the close of the navigable season, I
have little or no doubt that the pole of the
earth might easily be attained and passed, or a
direct course shaped towards Behring Strait;
and even, if all could not be effected in a single
season, steam power would lead us to a point
from which a voyage in the following year, would
be completed,—from whence an interesting portion of the polar features would be developed,—
and the problem solved upon which so many

valuable lives have been perilled and so many thousands of pounds expended.

In a geographic point of view this would indeed be interesting, but Baffin Bay, cannot, I think, ever be made a useful commercial route, while, on the other hand, I believe that a voyage might be readily undertaken and completed through the Spitzbergen Sea. But prejudice seems to have excluded, of late years, all idea of an attempt by this route, and yet I cannot but feel convinced, that the dying words of that great voyager Baffin deserve more consideration. He parted with his life on the scene of his last discoveries, declaring that he firmly believed had he kept a more middle course between Spitzbergen and Nova Zembla, that he would have passed into clear water and through the great Polynia of the Russians.

To those who may be inclined to ask, why did I not return to Smith Sound, after the gale had ceased which forced me to retire from it, on the 27th of August, a word of explanation is due.

A week previous to the attainment of our
most northern latitude I had been warned by
Mr. Abernethy, who had spent many winters
in the Arctic regions, that I had not more than
five or six days longer to navigate, as it was not
only essential that winter quarters should be
found, but every engagement made for entering
some place of safety at an hour's notice. To
prepare for this, the water had been pumped
out of the tanks and everything made ready,
but no spot could be observed where even an
anchorage could be obtained, and it must be
remembered, that much more than bare anchorage ground is necessary for laying a ship up for
the winter. Thus it was that when the gale
assailed our lonely barque, prudence pointed out
the necessity of retreating to the southward,
though I do think, that had fair winds favoured
another attempt, I could have resisted the temptation; but the reader will recollect that, instead of any such tempting change, a thick fog
and snow, with light variable winds, drove us
into the ice, and gave such an unpleasant fore-

taste of its iron grasp, that I believe the energies of all of us were a little damped, and that
snug quarters, rather than more adventure, were
wished for by all.

Female Esquimaux, Servant to the Governor at Fiskernœs.

TABLE SHOWING THE DEVIATION OF STANDARD COMPASS, 1852.

Isabel's Head at	ENGLAND. Greenhithe, 5th July.		GREENLAND. Hunde Islands, 4th October.		ENGLAND. Greenhithe, 25th Nov.		REMARKS, &c.
	° '	Direc- tion.	° '	Direc- tion.	° '	Direc- tion.	
NORTH.	2 45	E.	4 20	W.	3 40	W.	
N. by E.	3 57	E.	0 20	E.	1 22	W.	
N.N.E.	5 10	E.	4 20	E.	0 55	E.	
N.E. by N.	5 45	E.	7 20	E.	1 55	E.	It was found, after leaving Greenhithe, that an anvil and two mol-dols had been stowed under the coal within 10 feet of standard compass on the port side; these were of necessity removed, but no other alteration was made before the ship was swung at the Hunde Islands, in Greenland.
N.E.	6 20	E.	10 20	E.	2 55	E.	
N.E. by E.	6 5	E.	11 50	E.	4 25	E.	
E.N.E.	5 56	E.	13 20	E.	5 55	E,	
E. by N.	5 5	E.	14 0	E.	6 37	E.	
EAST.	4 20	E.	14 40	E.	7 20	E.	
E. by S.	2 40	E.	14 0	E.	5 45	E.	
E.S.E.	1 40	E.	13 20	E.	4 10	E.	It is most probable that the last deviations do not exhibit the maximum amount of deviation, in the most northern part of the voyage; but probably a table might be deduced showing its ratio to the increase of latitude.
S.E. by E.	0 20	E.	11 5	E.	3 10	E.	
S.E.	1 20	W.	8 50	E.	2 10	E.	
S.E. by S.	1 45	W.	6 30	E.	2 15	E.	
S.S.E.	2 25	W·	4 10	E.	2 10	E.	
S. by E.	2 42	W.	2 15	E.	1 42	E.	
SOUTH.	3 10	W.	0 20	E.	1 15	E.	
S. by W.	3 30	W.	2 40	W.	0 20	E.	At Hunde Islands the standard compass was taken on shore to observe the bearing of the island in line with the ship.
S.S.W.	3 50	W.	5 40	W.	0 35	W.	
S.W. by S.	4 12	W.	7 40	W.	0 47	W.	
S.W.	4 34	W.	9 40	W.	1 0	W.	A staff was placed in the centre of the position, over the compass stand.
S.W. by W.	4 56	W.	11 40	W.	1 55	W.	
W.S.W.	5 30	W.	13 40	W.	2 50	W.	
W. by S.	5 30	W.	16 15	W.	3 42	W.	
WEST..	5 50	W.	18 50	W.	4 35	W.	
W. by N.	6 10	W.	18 30	W.	5 37	W.	
W.N.W.	5 15	W.	18 10	W.	6 40	W.	
N.W. by W.	5 0	W.	17 25	W.	7 40	W.	
N.W.	4 40	W.	16 40	W.	8 40	W.	
N.W. by N.	3 0	W.	15 40	W.	7 52	W.	
N.N.W.	1 20	W.	10 30	W.	7 5	W.	
N. by W.	0 45	E.	7 35	W.	5 22	W.	

At Greenhithe, the ship was swung, with an observer on shore. And at Hunde Islands, by the bearing of an island, distant about 15 miles.

K

APPENDICES.

K 2

NOTES

ON

FLOWERING PLANTS AND ALGÆ,

COLLECTED DURING THE VOYAGE OF
THE "ISABEL."

By G. DICKIE, M.D.,

PROFESSOR OF NATURAL HISTORY, QUEEN'S COLLEGE, BELFAST.

NOTES ON FLOWERING PLANTS AND ALGÆ.

N.B.—The list of *Flowering Plants* has been compiled from a list by Sir W. J. Hooker, of species sent to him, and from a collection presented to myself by Dr. Sutherland.

DICOTYLEDONES.

Ranunculaceæ.

Ranunculus hyerboreus, *D. C.*   Disco Island.
R. nivalis, *Wahl.*   Wolstenholme Sound.
R. frigidus, *Willd.* . Wolstenholme Sound.

Papaveraceæ.

Papaver nudicaule, *L.*   Wolstenholme Sound.

Cruciferæ.

Cochlearia oblongifolia, *D. C.*   Disco Island and Wolsten-
holme Sound.
C. Grœnlandica, *L.*   Fiskernaes.
Draba alpina, *L.*   Whale Sound and Wolstenholme Sound.
D. hirta, *L.*   Whale Sound.
D. glacialis, *Adans.*   Whale Sound and Wolstenholme
Sound.

Caryophyllaceæ.

Stellaria media, *L.* Fiskernaes.
S. longipes, *Goldie.* Fiskernaes, Whale Sound, and Wolstenholme Sound.
Cerastium alpinum, *L.* Disco Island and Whale Sound.
C. latifolium, *L.* Disco Island.
Lychnis alpina, *L.* Fiskernaes.
L. apetala, *L.* Wolstenholme Sound and Whale Sound.

Rosaceæ.

Potentilla tridentata, *Ait.* Fiskernaes.
P. nivea, *L.* Whale Sound.
Dryas integrifolia, *L.* Fiskernaes.
Alchemilla alpina, *L.* Fiskernaes.

Onagraceæ.

Epilobium angustifolium, *L.* Fiskernaes.
E. latifolium, *L.* Fiskernaes.

Saxifragaceæ.

Saxifraga nivalis, *L.* Fiskernaes.
S. cæspitosa, *L.* Fiskernaes.
S. Aizóon, *L.* Fiskernaes.
S. cernua, *L.* Wolstenholme Sound.
S. tricuspidata, *D. C.* Wolstenholme and Whale Sounds.

Compositæ.

Hieracium murorum, *L.* Fiskernaes.
Gnaphalium sylvaticum, *L.* Fiskernaes.
Leontodon Taraxacum, *L.* Whale Sound.

Campanulaceæ.

Campanula rotundifolia, *L.* Fiskernaes.

Ericaceæ.

Menziesia cærulea, *Wall.* Fiskernaes.
Cassiope tetragona, *Don.* Wolstenholme Sound.
Ledum latifolium, *Ait.* Fiskernaes.
Loisleuria procumbens, *Desf.* Fiskernaes.

Pyrolaceæ.

Pyrola rotundifolia, *L.* Disco Island.

Vacciniaceæ.

Vaccinium uliginosum, *L.* Fiskernaes.

Scrophulariaceæ.

Bartsia alpina, *L.* Fiskernaes.
Euphrasia officinalis, *L.* Fiskernaes.
Pedicularis hirsuta, *L.* Wolstenholme Sound.

Labiatæ.

Thymus Serpyllum, *L.* Fiskernaes.

Polygonaceæ.

Polygonum viviparum, *L.* Fiskernaes, Disco Island, and
    Wolstenholme Sound.
Oxyria reniformis, *L.* Fiskernaes.
Kœnigia islandica, *L.* Disco Island.

138   APPENDIX.

Empetraceæ.

Empetrum nigrum, *L.*   Fiskernaes.

Betulaceæ.

Betula nana, *L.*   Fiskernaes.

Salicaceæ.

Salix arctica, *Pall.*   Fiskernaes and Whale Sound.
S. glauca, *L.*   Fiskernaes.
S. myrtilloides, *L.*   Fiskernaes.
S. herbacea, *L.*   Disco Island.

MONOCOTYLEDONES.

Orchidaceæ.

Habenaria albida, *Br.*   Fiskernaes.

Juncaceæ.

Juncus trifidus, *L.*   Fiskernaes.
Luzula spicata, *D. C.*   Fiskernaes.
L. campestris, *L.* (*var.* congesta)   Fiskernaes and Wolsten-
    holme Sound.

Cyperaceæ.

Eriophorum polystachyum, *L.*   Fiskernaes.
E. capitatum, *Schrad.*   Disco Island.
Carex cæspitosa, *Good.*   Fiskernaes.
C. exilis, *Dewey.*   Disco Island.
C. scirpoidea, *Mich.*   Disco Island.
C. rigida, *L.*   Disco Island.

Gramineæ.

Deyeuxia strigosa, *Kth.*   Fiskernaes.

Trisetum subspicatum, *Beauv.*   Fiskernaes.

Phippsia monandra, *Trin.*   Whale Sound and Wolstenholme
    Sound.

Poa alpina, *L.*   Fiskernaes and Wolstenholme Sound.

P. cænisia, *All.*   Fiskernaes.

P. cæsia, *Sm.*   Whale Sound.

P. laxa, *Hænke.*

P. arctica, *Pall.*

Alopecurus alpinus, *Sm.*   Whale Sound.

Agrostis rubra, *L.*   Fiskernaes.

Festuca ovina, *L.* (*var.* vivipara)   Fiskernaes.

Elymus arenarius, *L.*   Hunde Islands.

Filices.

Woodsia Iivensis, *Br.*   Fiskernaes.

A L G Æ.

MELANOSPERMEÆ.

Fucaceæ.

Fucus vesiculosus, *L.* Hunde Islands, 40 to 50 fathoms ;
   Whale Islands ; floating near Beechy Island ; on
   the beach, Whale Sound. The specimens nearly
   all destitute of vesicles.
F. nodosus, *L.* Fiskernaes and Whale Islands, and floating
   in 73° 50′ N.

Sporochnaceæ.

Desmarestia viridis, *Lam.* Hunde Islands, 50 to 100
   fathoms.
D. aculeata, *Lam.* Fiskernaes ; Hunde Islands; 80 to 100
   fathoms ; Whale Islands ; floating in lat. 73° 20′ N.

Laminariaceæ.

Alaria esculenta, *Grev.* On the beach, Whale Sound. It
   attains a large size even in such high latitudes,
   some of the fronds being upwards of six inches
   broad.
Laminaria Fascia, *Ag.* Hunde Islands, in 40 to 50 fathoms.
L. saccharina, *Lam.* Hunde Islands, in 50 to 100 fathoms.

L. longicruris, *De la Pyl.* Melville Bay ; Whale Sound ;
Cape Saumarez ; specimens found floating off Dark
Head, coast of West Greenland, lat 72° 15′ N.,
must have been upwards of 10 feet in length, their
roots abounding in animal forms peculiar to deep
water.

L. digitata, *Lam.* Whale Sound.

Agarum Turneri, *Post.* and *Rupr.* Hunde Islands, in 10 to
100 fathoms ; Whale Island, in 40 to 50 fathoms ;
Melville Bay.

Dictyotyaceæ.

Dictyota Fasciola, *Lam.* Hunde Islands, in 40 to 50 fathoms ;
Whale Islands, 20 to 40 fathoms.

Dictyosiphon fæniculaceus, *Grev.* Hunde Islands, in 50 to
70 fathoms ; and floating in lat. 73° 20′ N.

Asperococcus Turneri, *Hook.* Fiskernaes.

Chordariaceæ.

Chordaria flagelliformis, *Ag.* Fiskernaes ; Hunde Islands,
40 to 100 fathoms ; Whale Islands ; Melville Bay.

Elachista fucicola, *Fries.* Fiskernaes ; Whale Islands.

E. flaccida, *Aresch* (?) On Desmarestia aculeata, Whale
Islands.

Myrionema strangulans, *Grev.* A minute plant, probably
identical with this species, was found infesting
Callithamnion Rothii, at low-water mark, Hunde
Islands.

Ectocarpaceæ.

Chætopteris plumosa, *Kutz.* Hunde Islands, 25 to 30
fathoms ; on the beach, Whale Sound.

Ectocarpus littoralis, *Lyngb.* Fiskernaes ; Hunde Islands,
50 to 100 fathoms ; and floating in lat. 73° 20′ N.

E. Durkeei, *Harv.* (?) Fragments, apparently of this species, mixed with the following.

E. Landsburgii, *Harv.*   Hunde Islands, in 70 to 80 fathoms.

RHODOSPERMEÆ.

Rhodomelaceæ.

Polysiphonia nigrescens, *Grev.*   Fragments, apparently of this variable species, were found at Hunde Islands in 40 to 50 fathoms ; and cast up in Whale Sound.

Corallinaceæ.

Melobesia polymorpha, *Linn.*   Erebus and Terror Bay, in 15 fathoms.

M. fasciculata, *Harv.*   Erebus and Terror Bay, in 8 to 10 fathoms.

M. lichenoides, *Borl.*   At low-water mark, Fiskernaes ; Hunde Islands, 7 fathoms ; Cape Adair, 12 to 18 fathoms.

Sphærococcoideæ.

Delesseria sinuosa, *Lam.*   Dark Head.

D. angustissima, *Griff.*   Whale Islands.

Calliblepharis ciliata, *Kutz.*   On the beach, Whale Islands.

Squamarieæ.

Peyssonnelia Dubyi, *Crouan.*   Cape Adair, in 12 to 15 fathoms, on stones.

Rhodymeniaceæ.

Euthora cristata, *J. Ag.*   Hunde Islands, 90 to 100 fathoms.

Cryptonemiaceæ.

Callophyllis laciniata, *Kutz.* Whale Islands, floating and
cast on the beach.
Halosaccion ramentaceum, *J. Ag.* Whale Islands, cast up.

Ceramiaceæ.

Ptilota serrata, *Kutz.* Whale Islands, 30 to 40 fathoms ;
Whale Sound, floating.
Callithamnion Rothii, *Lyngb.* Hunde Islands, at low-water
mark : Cape Adair, on stones, dredged in 12 to 18
fathoms.

CHLOROSPERMEÆ.

Confervaceæ.

Cladophora Inglefieldii, *N. S.* Low-water mark, Fiskernaes.
C. rupestris, *Kg.* Low-water mark, Fiskernaes.
C. arcta, *Kg.* Low-water mark, Fiskernaes.
C. uncialis, *Harv.* Omenak and Whale Sound.
Conferva Melagonium, *Web.* and *Mohr.* Cape Bowen, Whale
Sound, and Beechy Island.
C. Fragments of a species probably near C. Youngana. Cape
Bowen, Hunde Islands, 25 to 30 fathoms.
C. capillaris, *L.* Fresh-water pools, Hunde Islands.
C. bombycina, *Ag.* In pools, Hunde Islands.

Ulvaceæ.

Enteromorpha intestinalis, *Link.* Hunde Islands and Cape
Bowen.
E. percursa, *Hook.* On the beach at Hunde Islands.

Ulva latissima, *Linn.*   Low-water mark, Omenak.
U. crispa, *Lightf.* Whale Islands.
Porphyra vulgaris, *Ag.*   Whale Sound.

Nostochineæ.

Nostoc sphæricum, *Vauch.*   In fresh-water pools, Hunde
    Islands.

Diatomaceæ.

Fragments of a minute species of Schizonema, too imperfect
    for recognition, were found on drift wood, in lat.
    62° N. long. 51° W.; also on stones, at Cape
    Bowen and Whale Sound.

A FEW REMARKS

ON THE

PHYSICAL GEOGRAPHY, &c.,

OF

DAVIS STRAITS, AND ITS EAST AND WEST SHORES.

BY

P. C. SUTHERLAND,

SURGEON TO THE EXPEDITION.

A FEW REMARKS,

&c., &c.

THE coasts of Davis Straits and Baffin Bay, stretching northward from Cape Farewell on the eastern, and Cape Walsingham on the western shore, to Sir Thomas Smith Sound, deserve, from their extent alone, the attention of the geographer; the countless inhabitants of the seas washing these coasts, from the huge Greenland whale to the beautifully striated diatoma of microscopic minuteness, afford to the zoologist much work for many years to come; and the character of the rocks comprising so large a section of our earth, is to the geologist a matter of at least ordinary importance. The chief interest of these regions to the latter, however, does not reside exclusively in the mere character of the different formations he may discover, for,

L 2

by following and minutely observing the daily
action of glaciers, icebergs, and coast-ice, upon
these formations, he will be assisted very materi-
ally in determining the action by which great
changes were wrought, in bygone epochs, upon
the crust of our planet, and thus he will be
enabled to trace out the analogy of well known
agents now at work with extinct but somewhat
similar agents, the results of which are at best
a good deal problematical. The Alps and
Himmalaya, begirt with the line of eternal snow,
and affording passage through their narrow
gorges to the slowly descending glacier, are each
visited by him that he may, on the spot, behold
the disintegrating and abrading action of water,
assisted by alternating heat and cold, and also
that he may judge of its power to convey from
distant and inaccessible mountain heights to
fertile valleys and level plains great accumulations of rock in the form of large fragments,
pebbles, sand, and fine mud. The quantity of
earthy and saline matter carried by our rivers
into the ocean is estimated with great care for
the purpose of ascertaining the rate of increase
of deposits now taking place, and to what extent
the sea is encroaching upon the land by the dis-
placement of water resulting from this introduc-

tion of foreign matter. The breakers wearing down our coasts and shallowing the immediately adjoining seas with the strewed fragments of the cliffs, be they hard or soft, are closely watched in their levelling progress by the student of nature, and he probably looks forward with prophetic vision to the far distant day in which the greatest part of this island, and much of the whole world, will have passed from under the feet of men into the troubled waters of the ocean. And the direction and force of the currents of the ocean, the circulatory system of the universe, in increasing or diminishing the temperature of continents according as they flow towards or from the Poles, are made subjects of deep research. If, then, each of these natural phenomena require undivided attention, surely that part of the world in which all of them work together in the most perfect harmony does so in an especial manner.

The Danish settlers in West Greenland have pretty accurately laid down the geographical character of the coast from Cape Farewell to Cape Shakleton, about lat. 74°. Beyond this latitude, however, as far as $78\frac{1}{2}°$, the highest point yet attained in Baffin Bay, and down along the west coast of Davis Straits as far as

Cumberland and Frobisher Straits, it is less perfectly known from the difficulty experienced in approaching it by the whaling and discovery ships—the only ships that ever attempt to reach it.

Commencing with Cape Farewell, there is no difficulty in at once referring the rocks to the crystalline formations from the rugged and peaked outline of the coast presented to the navigator as he advances towards it from the eastward. Here, as in most parts of the same coast and many other parts of the icy regions, the coast is intersected by fiords of great length, in which the tide is generally very rapid and the water is of considerable depth; and it appears as if composed of a chain of islands, varying much in size and clustering together in front of the vast glacier continent of Greenland. Proceeding northward, at Disco Island, on the 70th parallel of latitude, we find an appearance of coast altogether different. Viewing this island from a distance of ten miles to seaward, it presents a succession of steps, and appears to be made up of a number of truncated cones, planted so closely together that the bases of all of them meet, some at the level of the sea, bounding long and winding valleys, and others at every intermediate point, until the highest point is reached at, probably an elevation of four to six thousand feet. Such a contour is at once suggestive of volcanic origin. At the northern extremity of this island hypogenous rocks occur, from the sea level to an elevation of about one hundred feet. The settlement of Godhaven, or Leively, is on this part of the island, from which, at a distance of only one or two miles to the northward, the tufaceous formation can be discerned, overlying the harder and more primitive rocks. In South-east Bay, ten to twenty miles southward of Disco, a number of islands are observed in several groups, which, from their general appearance and from specimens collected on the spot, evidently partake of the crystalline character of the south end of this island.

From the researches of Dr. Rink, an enterprising Danish traveller, we learn that coal and sandstone are abundantly met with on the south-east and north-east shores of Disco Island, the north side of the Waigat Strait, the south shore of Omenak's Fiorde, Hare Island, and an island in North-east Bay, and in the coast on the 72nd parallel, a few miles southward of the settlement of Proven. Of the purity of this coal, and of its value as fuel, we may judge from the following analysis, which was performed by Professor Fyfe, of King's College, Aberdeen, upon a specimen sent home from Disco Island, by some of the officers of Sir Edward Belcher's expedition.

Its specific gravity is 1·3848.

Volatile matter	50·6
Coke, consisting of ash . . . 9·84	
Fixed carbon . . . . 39·56	
	49·4
	100·

As I never had an opportunity of visiting the coal-bearing localities, the necessary detail with respect to direction, extent, and thickness of beds, cannot be entered into at present.

At Cape Cranstoune, situate on the north side of North-east Bay, the trap formation peculiar to Disco Island occurs, and extends northward apparently in one unbroken vein as far as Proven, in lat. 72° 20′, or thereabout. Here we find the volcanic rocks interrupted, and northward, to Cape York, lat. 76°, with one or two slight exceptions in lat. 73° 20′ and 74°, numerous islands, and every part of the coast that protrudes from beneath the glacier, are composed of gneiss and granite. At Cape York, and on to Cape Atholl, thirty to forty miles farther north, although differing

in outline by the glacial accumulation from
Disco Island, and other well known parts of the
coast to the southward, the rocks can be referred
with unquestionable certainty to the same
volcanic origin. Northward of the last mentioned Cape, in the entrance of Wolstenholme
Sound, we find a flat island, (called Saunders
Island, out of compliment to the commander of
H.M.S. "North Star," which ship wintered
near it in 1849-50,) which, from its distinctly
stratified appearance, suggests the commence-
ment of a different series of rocks, or at least a
slight interruption to those of igneous character.
Eastward of Cape Atholl, on the south shore of
the sound, the strata are seen cropping out, with
a dip to the south-west.   This dip is at variance
with what we observe in Saunders Island, where
the strata are perfectly horizontal. At Omenak,
the native settlement, in the sound, and the
reported scene of the destruction by fire of
Franklin's ships and of the murder of their
crews, a calcareous sandstone, with a dip of about
15° to west-south-west, occurs interstratified
with greenstone ; and immediately to the westward of the settlement, Mount Dundas, a tabulated hill of very striking appearance, is probably
composed of materials of the same igneous origin
as the latter. The unconformable condition of

the secondary or deposition strata and their asso-
ciation in such intimate relation with volcanic
rocks, prepares us for what we observe as we
advance northward. At the top of Wolstenholme Sound, in the same bluff, the strata,
dipping about south-west, vary from 10° to 25°
or 30°. In Granville Bay, about twenty miles
farther north, they vary considerably, occurring
sometimes nearly perfectly horizontal, and
again with an angle of 45° in several directions.
In the entrance of this bay several small islands
occur, which, from their rough and dark appearance, together with the depth of the water
around, as indicated by the size of the icebergs
seen close to them, we may safely put down as
volcanic. Towards Cape Parry, and but a few
miles southward of it, in Booth Sound, a remarkable bell-shaped rock, (Fitzclarence Rock,)
of a dark colour, and apparently exceedingly
hard, rises in an isolated form to a height of
probably five or six hundred feet out of a comparatively level plain, the seaward continuation
of one or more of the numerous taluses in the
neighbourhood. To this, even in the entire
absence of specimens, may be safely assigned
the igneous character of the small islands already
noticed.

From Cape Parry eastward to Bardin Bay,

in the south shore of Whale Sound, the strata incline a little to the westward, and they are in many places somewhat curved. Still further to the eastward they are partly conformable with a dip of about 30° to south-west, and they are frequently intersected by irregular dikes of igneous rocks, which are of a very dark colour when viewed from a distance of five or six miles. One of these dikes rises in the form of an angry looking peak above the outline of the other strata, and in the entrance of Bardin Bay, the ship drawing ten to twelve feet of water, struck upon a rock, which, from the depth of the water (fifty to sixty fathoms) within a couple of hundred yards, I consider to be a second protrusion of the same rocks above the contour of the deposition strata at the bottom. At a point on the east side of Bardin Bay we recognized the same calcareous sandstone observed at Omenak, sixty miles to the southward, occurring in unconformable and somewhat curved strata, inclining west-south-west, at an angle of 15°. A specimen picked up from the brow of the hill above this point, at no great distance from one of the trap dikes, appears to be a sort of porphyritic greenstone.

In other parts of Whale Sound, as we can

judge from the appearance of portions of Northumberland, Herbert, and Milne Islands, the deposition strata are perfectly horizontal. And at Cape Saumarez in the same coast, but thirty miles north of this sound, the same strata can be traced from one cliff to another, in conformable and horizontal lines over many miles.

At Cape Alexander, the eastern boundary of the entrance of Sir Thomas Smith's Sound, in latitude 78° 15', we again find the strata a little curved ; but only a few miles farther north they are so regular in parallelism and succession, as to vie with a distant view of the Crystal Palace, with the name of which Captain Inglefield has honoured one of the bluffs, and thus perpetuated in the icy north the recollection of that memorable although only temporary edifice. In the absence of specimens, for we had no opportunity of landing, and of highly characteristic outlines, the nature of the remaining part of the coast northward of the Exhibition Cliffs, and of a small island close to Cape Alexander, must be left to be determined by future explorers ; the island however seems to be composed of a very rough-grained light-coloured sandstone, probably similar to that found at Bardin Bay, Whale Sound.

The west shore of Smith's Sound, from Victoria

Head, beyond the 79th degree of latitude to
Cape Isabella, and the coast leading northward
to Jones' Sound, is so inapproachable from the
drifting pack-ice in the season for navigation,
that I fear we will not soon have specimens of
the rocks by which to determine the character
of so large a portion of the coast. And it is
everywhere so covered by the glacial accumulation, that the outlines of only mere protrusions
of the land, taken from distances of ten to twenty
miles, scarcely afford the materials for correct
results. From its greater height in many parts
than the adjacent shore, and also from its rugged,
in some cases even pinnacled contour, thus resembling the coast at Cape Farewell, the idea of
fossiliferous strata may safely be excluded.

The north shore of Jones' Sound, from Cape
Clarence to Pickthorne Bay, appears in outline
to resemble a tufaceous formation. But I
suspect it and the south shore from Cape Fitzroy
westward into the Trenter Mountains, together
with Coburg and Leopold Islands, and Princess
Charlotte's Monument in the entrance of Jones'
Sound, are all one hypogenous formation, continuous with that already indicated northward of
Cape Clarence to Victoria Head. From Cape
Fitzroy southward to Hyde Bay, the coast

appears to partake of the same primitive character. But at the latter locality, one or two
tabulated hills occur with undulating slopes,
which seem to be either a secondary probably
fossiliferous formation or trap, assuming at the
distance from which we observed it a distinctly
stratified appearance. From these table hills to
Cape Warrender and westward to Croker Bay,
on the north shore of Lancaster Sound, there is
a slight resemblance with Disco Island; this,
however, is not sufficient to refer so large a
portion of the coast to the same igneous agency
as that island ; although, there need be no doubt
of its non-fossiliferous character.

On the opposite shore of Lancaster Sound,
at Cape Walter Bathurst, the crystalline rocks
are again recognized, and from this point southward they form the whole coast, with, so far as
my knowledge goes, only one exception, near
Cape Walsingham, where coal has been found
by the whaling ships. The islands in and on
both sides of Cumberland Straits, of Baffin, and
Hudson, or Hogarth Sound, of Penny on the
64th and 65th degrees of latitude, are chiefly,
so far as that unexplored part has been examined,
composed of primitive and metamorphic rocks.
At Kingaite, a large inlet on its north side

leading in the direction of Cape Walsingham, from the appearance of the land at a distance of several miles, I am disposed to think that there is an interruption of tufaceous or erupted matter to the crystalline series. If this is proved to be correct by subsequent observers we shall then be in a position to draw comparisons, and to form analogies between the geological characters of the east and west shores of Davis Straits and Baffin Bay.

The extensive primitive formation indicated in these remarks, to extend from Victoria Head, about latitude 79° to Cape Enderby, latitude 63°, on the side of Cumberland Straits, is flanked to the westward by an equally, if not much more extensive formation, of silurian rocks, the limits of which as yet we have been quite unable to ascertain. The chief, indeed, in the present state of our knowledge, it may be said, the only navigable channel through which the latter has been reached is Lancaster Sound ; it is probable, however, we may find it continuous to the westward with the American series of the same rocks. Through the labours of Mr. König and Professor Jameson, thirty years ago, and of Mr. Salter only very recently, some of the points peculiar to North Somerset, North Devon, and

the North Georgian Islands, have been described
from the fragmentary specimens brought home
by the ships engaged in the discovery of these
places during the last thirty years.*

In the vicinity of Cape Farewell, at Julianas
Haab, I believe, some ore of *copper* has been
found by the Danes, but only in small quantity.
And northward to Upper Navik, in the same
coast, *graphite* of tolerable purity occurs in considerable abundance. The Danish settlers have
not yet begun to work out on an extensive scale
the sources of the latter, nor will they permit
us on any terms to do so ; this, however, is of
less importance, from the fact that on the opposite side of Davis Straits, in Cumberland Straits
or Hogarth Sound, about the 65th degree of
latitude the same valuable mineral is found of
equal purity and abundance.

It is rather a striking coincidence, that in the

* Parry's Voyages in Search of a North-west Passage.—
Sutherland's Journal of Penny's Voyage in Search of Sir
John Franklin.

Note.—The Rev. Mr. Longmuir, of Aberdeen, found
numerous specimens of the genus *Rhynconella* in the ballast
of the "Prince Albert," a ship recently returned from Batty
Bay, Prince Regent's Inlet, on the east shore of North
Somerset, thus proving undeniably the presence of the
Silurian series of rocks in that locality.

north part of the eastern and western hemi-
spheres, we should find indications of both
elevation and subsidence of the land. The extensive researches of Sir Charles Lyall prove
that these wonderful phenomena have occurred
in the north of Europe, and those of Dr. Pingel
and Captain Graah, in Greenland, leave no
doubt that the east coast of that icy continent
is gradually subsiding.* The tertiary deposits of
the extensive fossiliferous region westward of
Lancaster Sound, occurring at every elevation
from the sea level to probably 1,000 feet, the
greatest height attained by any part of the land
in that tract, marked by raised beaches and
abounding in shells found alive in the present
day in the surrounding seas, suggest the idea
with an unmistakeable meaning of a gradual
upheaval. It is difficult to conclude whether,
the deposition of the calcareous sandstone and
the eruption of the submarine volcanic matter
found in West Greenland is contemporaneous
with that of the fossiliferous strata, five hundred
miles to the westward ; the probability, however,
cannot be denied, that the accumulation of the
detritus of the latter strata, containing as it does
marine shells, took place at a period subsequent

* Principles of Geology, Seventh Edition, chap. xxxi.

M

to the elevation of the former from beneath the
ocean. On the Greenland side we find immense
boulders of gneiss and granite resting on islands
and parts of the coast, which present quite a
different structure from that of the rocks supporting them. This is a good proof that icebergs alone, previous to the elevation of the
Greenland coast, could have dropped them upon
their resting places. On the undulating slopes
and along the raised beaches of the North
Georgian group, and North Devon, we also find
travelled materials, such as fragments of greenstone, quartz, and anthracite, serpentine gneiss,
granite, but of such small size that we at once
refer their mode of conveyance not to icebergs
but to coast-ice, such as in the present day
occupies the comparatively shallow seas in the
various inlets and channels leading from the
western extremity of Lancaster Sound. If, then,
these two regions differ in the present day, by
the one undergoing subsidence while the other is
moving in an opposite direction, or is at least in
a state of apparent permanency, they also differ
with respect to the physical agents peculiar to
each in by-gone epochs. This leads the attention to glacial action, which is of vast importance to the geologist and physical geographer.

At Cape Farewell, the fiords run so far into the interior that not one of the icebergs escaping into them from the glacier ever reaches Davis Straits, and if the navigator meets with these floating masses in the neighbourhood of this promontory, they must have drifted to it from other sources. As we advance northward along the coast of West Greenland, and thus diminish the annual mean temperature both of the sea and of the atmosphere, we find the glacier approaches nearer and nearer the coast-line, until in Melville Bay, latitude 75°, it presents to the sea one continuous wall of ice, unbroken by land for a space of probably seventy or eighty miles. To the southward of Melville Bay there are numerous outlets in the coast for the ice, and they vary in breadth from two or three up to fifteen to twenty miles. To have a correct idea of the glacier accumulation in Greenland, we must imagine a continent of ice protected on its seaward side by a number of islands, and lost to vision in every other direction as one boundless and continuous plain. This is remarkably well shown in the map accompanying Dr. Rink's work.* Through the spaces between these islands,

* De Danske Handelsdisihkter, I. Nord, Grœnland, Af H. Rink.

M 2

" the gathered winter of a thousand years"
slowly seeks its passage to the sea, and sends
off an annual tribute of icebergs to encumber,
to cool, and to dilute the waters of the adjoining
ocean. The average height or depth of the ice
at its free edge in these valleys is about twelve
or fifteen hundred feet, of which I believe one-
eighth or one hundred and fifty feet will be
above water. In some of the valleys, however,
the depth is upwards of two thousand four hundred feet. This may be considered to be satisfactorily ascertained, for the Esquimaux around
South-east Bay, latitude 68°, while pursuing
their fishing avocations during the winter
months, require lines of three hundred fathoms
to reach the bottom at the foot of the glacier in
the vicinity of Claushaven.

In South-east and also in North-east Bay, we
meet with the ice that draws the greatest depth of
water; but those of Melville Bay and of several
of the smaller bays immediately to the southward of it are of the greatest cubic contents.
At Cape York, in latitude 76°, although the
glacier is the northward continuation of the
glacier in Melville Bay, its protrusions into the
sea never exceed fifty to sixty feet above the
sea level; and in some places it does not enter

the sea in a continuous mass; but having descended over the cliffs it breaks off and slips down into the water over the rocks, which thus become scratched and scored in a remarkable manner. This is well seen at Cape Fitzroy, on the south side of Jones' Sound, and at Cape Bowen, on the south side of Pond's Bay, where the free edge of the ice is about fifty feet thick, and at least two hundred feet above the sea level, which with a tolerable slope would make a surface of, I should say, three hundred feet in breadth, over which the scoring process might extend. It is somewhat interesting to the geologist to observe this powerful abrading action; it would be a mistake, however, to consider it generally applicable, for although many hundred (I may safely state several thousand) miles of coast intersected by glaciers were examined in this voyage of the "Isabel," the cited localities, with one or two trifling exceptions, were the only places where it was observed. I believe it can be accounted for so far by the steepness of the inclination, but chiefly by the ice having become more friable (less plastic) from the diminished temperature; it is probable also the thickness or depth of the ice may take an important part in developing this interesting feature. One cannot easily determine why the icebergs that come from the glaciers at and to the northward of Cape York, and on the west side of Davis Straits and Baffin Bay are generally of less dimensions than elsewhere. At Cape York, where we have a new formation of rocks commencing, and farther northward in the same coast, it is probably owing to the comparative shallowness of the valleys, and to a diminished supply of snow from the greater intensity of the cold. On the west coast, from Victoria Head to Jones' Sound, although the land has almost a perfectly icy casing, the icebergs that are sent off are by no means large, and this, as so far in the other case, may arise from the decrease of vapour with the decrease of temperature. Again, from this sound southward, there cannot be such extensive accumulations of ice as on the opposite and more northern shore of the straits, although the rocks in both cases are of the same crystalline nature, for the reason, I believe, that the vapour-bearing stratum of air coming from the northward over an extensive tract of land, yields but scantily to the growth of the glacier on the former as compared with the latter. But it baffles still more to account for the entire absence of glacier on the silurian formation westward of Lancaster Sound. Why the snow and rain, falling on the land around Barrow Straits and its tributary inlets and bays, should all escape into the sea in running streams every year during the two short months of July and August, while that falling on the coasts of Davis Straits makes its escape as hard but yielding ice after a lapse of many ages, is a question worthy the deepest attention of the student of nature. The annual mean temperature in the creeks and inlets of Barrow Straits is several degrees lower than that in corresponding latitudes on the shores of Davis Straits ; and even at Wolstenholme Sound, nearly two degrees farther north, the annual mean temperature is three degrees higher than at Melville Island. This comparison of annual mean temperature will not throw any light upon our difficulty. The ranges of temperature will probably prove more useful. A few degrees up or down about the freezing point of water would settle the question. We know that the sea exerts a wonderful influence in rendering the climate temperate, as well as reducing the ranges of temperature. Where there is the greatest extent of water, be it fresh or salt, there the annual mean is greatest and the ranges are least.

Upon this theory, which has been so ably proved to be correct, by Sir Charles Lyall, the summer in the neighbourhood of Barrow Straits ought to be hotter than in Davis Straits, in the same latitude. And such we find it, as far as our limited observations in them can be made available. The month of July, 1851, at Cornwallis Island, was found to be three degrees warmer than the same month of the preceding year, in a corresponding latitude, on the east side of Davis Straits. This difference is but slight, however, it is on the favourable side, and when we associate with it the highly animalized character of the land, and also the diminished supply of vapour during the winter months, we have an approximation to the true cause why the glacier preponderates so largely in one direction, while it is entirely absent in another.

The travels of Professor J. Forbes and of Agassiz, in the Alps, have so fully established the true theory of the descent of glaciers, despite the apparent difference between the regions they visited and Greenland, as to render any remarks here almost altogether unnecessary. The introduction of extraneous matter into the substance of the ice to be borne along must be the same in every country. And so also must

be the deposition of moraines where the glacier
begins to protrude beyond the land, whether they
occur at the sea-level or at turnings at higher
elevations. This deposition of earthy matter
arises from the decay of the ice, rich in such
material, consequent upon free exposure to the
action of the sun, and it was remarkably well
seen at the south side of the Petowak glacier,
in the neighbourhood of Cape Atholl, both at
the sea level and at an angle two miles farther
up the side of the glacier. The concentric and
wavy appearance, so often noticed to be peculiar
to the surface of the glaciers in the Alps, is well
exemplified in the vicinity of Cape Saumarez
and of Cape Alexander. Professors Forbes and
Agassiz agree in attributing the roughness and
irregularity of the surface to the inequalities of
the bottom over which it has to pass, and more
especially if the action of the sun has not been
distributed irregularly by means of extraneous
matter. The concentric lines and wavy appearance above adverted to are scarcely to be attributed by these observers to the inequalities of
the bottom ; the other irregularities, however,
such as "crevasses," and extensive "faults"
can be referred to no other source, although it
must be confessed that the relation of sympathy

cannot be very powerful which appears to exist between the lower and upper surfaces of such a plastic mass as a glacier, apart as they are in some cases upwards of two thousand feet. That there is this sympathy and relation, however small or limited they may be in their operation, there need be no doubt, for, in many icebergs we often observe crevasses extending throughout all of their length and breadth that is visible, which have become so filled with mud and extraneous matter as to be discernible at a distance of many miles ; and these crevasses could not have occurred at any time or under any circumstances except during the descent of the glacier. The glacier of Petowak, and another glacier of small size near Cape Fitzroy, shew the crevasses and faults, or slips in great perfection. There is, however, a peculiarly pinnacled condition of the upper surface of many magnificent icebergs and extensive glaciers which cannot possibly be attributed to inequality at the bottom, and many icebergs and glaciers of very large size, as well as small, are so flat and smooth in the upper surface that one can hardly conceive any rocky bottom to be equally smooth, torn up, as it cannot fail to be, by glacial action. On the north side of Clarence Head, in the north shore of

Jones' Sound, I observed that one portion of the surface of a flat but extensive glacier that protruded several miles into the sea was exceedingly smooth, while another portion of it was so minutely rough and pinnacled that to have walked over it would have been quite impossible. We must assign this roughness either to some peculiar atmospheric influence, or to the difference of temperature between the surface and the interior of the glacier, together with a downward motion. Eight feet is the thickness to which a minimum temperature of − 45°, a monthly mean of − 30°, or an annual mean temperature of + 2·5, extended the freezing point of water through fresh water ice on a lake in lat. 74° 40′ north, and lon. 94° 16′ west ; the greatest depth of the water in the lake being only two fathoms. If we can presume the conducting power of ice formed on the surface of water and of glacier ice to be the same, then the temperature of the glacier below the above depth with the same minimum or mean annual degree of cold, would be + 32°. The surface exposed to every alternation of heat and cold, from the freezing point to − 45°, or possibly many degrees lower, would necessarily become contorted and disturbed by contraction and expansion, even suppose the bodies supporting it were standing still. But when we reflect that the latter retains its plasticity and continues its downward motion, it need not be wondered that the former, hard and brittle, assumes a broken up appearance. This view, however, does not quite satisfy us for the reason that it is not universally applicable.

Following the example of Mr. Christie, one of the secretaries of the Royal Society,[*] during a winter in Barrow Straits, I performed a number of experiments by submitting water, in a strong iron bottle, to various temperatures, from $+30°$ to $-45°$. The result of such exposure was, as a matter of course, congelation of the water, accompanied by the usual expansion, in which a column of ice rose through the orifice of the bottle to a height in proportion to the quantity of water used, and the dimensions of the orifice. While the temperature did not descend more than eight or ten degrees below the freezing point, the column of ice ascending through the orifice or "fuze hole," and always amounting to about one-tenth of the whole mass of water,

* Sir Charles Lyall's Principles of Geology. Seventh Edition, p. 226.

retained its cohesive property in such perfection that, without being broken, and although only half an inch in diameter, the whole apparatus, weighing four or five pounds could be raised, and sometimes even inverted by its means.   But at lower temperatures the ice escaped with a crepitating sound, and frequently with explosive reports, accompanied each by a sudden rejection or propulsion of a portion of it to a distance of several feet ; it was so friable, too, that it separated into discs, half or a quarter of an inch in thickness, and sometimes crumbled into fragments among the fingers.

The important points contested some years ago by Professors J. Forbes and Mr. Hopkins come within this field of research. They are well known, and need not be recounted here.   From what has been observed in the Alps, it may be considered a settled question, that the downward motion of glaciers is constant, and unaffected by low temperatures applied to the surface, especially when the thickness or depth of the solid ice amounts to a great number of feet.   In the Alps, and even within the tropics, although it may appear strange to contemplate glaciers in the latter region, they travel great distances from the snow and ice-clad heights until gradu-

ally they descend to and perhaps beyond the
regions habitable by man, where they undergo
dissolution by the increase of temperature.   In
Greenland, after descending to the sea through
the valleys, they retain their hold of the partu-
rient womb beyond until the buoyant properties
of ice come into operation, and then they give
birth to icebergs of sometimes inconceivable dimensions.   The constant rise and fall of the tide
exerts great power in detatching these floating
ice-islands.   By it a hinge-like action is set up
as soon as the glacier comes within its influence,
and is carried on although the surface of the
sea for many leagues around is covered with one
continuous sheet of ice.   After summer has set
in and advanced somewhat, the surface-ice either
drifts or melts away, and we have winds prevailing in a direction contrary to what they had
been during the cold season of the year, and the
result of these winds is a great influx of water
into Davis Straits, causing tides unusual for
height at other seasons of the year, and thus
setting at liberty whole fields of icebergs, which
then commence their slow southward course.
In August, 1850, the number set free in a deep
fiorde, near Omenak, North-east Bay, so occupied
the navigable passage out of the harbour at that

settlement that the Danish ship, which had but a month previously entered the harbour with perfect safety, was in danger of being detained for the winter. In the same month of 1852, the whole of the coast southward of Melville Bay to Uppernavik, extending over a space of 180 miles in length, and probably twelve to fifteen in breadth, was rendered perfectly unnavigable by any means whatever; and when we sailed along this portion of the coast, about the middle of the month, we were astounded, not disagreeably, by the constant booming sounds that issued from whole fields of these wonder working agents while undergoing their frolicsome revolutions. To me there appeared to be a remarkable change in this locality, for, two years previously, in the months of June and July, a whole fleet of large ships occupied and navigated the very place which now we could no more enter and navigate with the ship than navigate her through the City of London, half submerged in the sea, and all the houses tumbling about and butting each other as they would do in an earthquake. At Cape York, this season, in a semicircle of twelve miles, one could count nearly two hundred icebergs, all apparently newly detatched from the glacier.

And in the top of Wolstenholme Sound, the
icebergs that had come off from the three pro-
truding points of the glacier entering it, were so
closely planted together that it was not without
some difficulty and danger that we advanced
among them, although aided by steam.

The effects of bodies of such vast dimensions
and numbers on the rocks at the bottom must
be as extensive as they are important. While
passing up the Straits early in the season, one
does not often see sea weed floating on the
surface of the water, but at a period somewhat
later, after these natural reapers have sallied out
to mow down their harvests, we meet with whole
rafts of the produce of the submarine forests in
these regions, floating abundantly down the
straits. The stems of laminaria are often found
abraded, and their roots contain shells, star-
fishes, (solaster— ?), and other animals, some,
indeed many of which, like the plants that
floated them to the surface, have suffered from
the powerful action that set them free. In no
part of Davis Straits, from Cape Farewell to
Smith's Sound, on either side, or mid-channel,
from two to two hundred fathoms, wherever the
dredge has reached the bottom, there animals
have been found to exist, in spite of iceberg

action, in its most intense form, upon their muddy or rocky habitats. Ascidians and cirrhipeds, and many other animals which attach themselves to the rocks at considerable depths, are often brought up. The Echinoderms, which we know are too slow in their motions to escape danger, swarm in the utmost profusion in these seas. The sea-urchin (*Echinus neglectus*), and several genera of brittle-stars have been found in Melville Bay, at depths varying from 90 up to 200 fathoms. And the same creatures, together with many others, among which may be recognized the genera *Terebratula, Mya, Saxicava, Mytilus, Cardium,* (perhaps *Venericardia,*) *Pecten, Astarte, Leda, Nucula, Lima, Natica, Scutaria, Chiton, Patella, Fissurella,* besides great varieties of *Corallines, Serpulæ,* &c., have also been found at various depths, from two to one hundred fathoms, among the Hunde Islands in North-east Bay, where icebergs abundantly float about and often take the ground. Some of the larger shells taken up were a good deal broken up, and not unfrequently deposits of their finely divided detritus were discovered by means of the dredge.

Except from the evidence thus afforded by plants and animals at the bottom, we have no

N

means whatever to ascertain the effects produced
by icebergs upon the rocks.   Doubtless, when
these powerful agents contain earthy matter they
must scratch and groove the rocks at the bottom
" as the diamond cuts the glass," and when they
are impelled along a muddy bottom they cannot
fail to raise moraines and leave deep depressions
in its otherwise smooth surface.   But it will be
well to bear in mind that when an iceberg
touches the ground, if that ground is hard and
resisting, it must come to a stand ; the propel-
ling power continuing a slight leaning over in
the water or yielding motion of the whole mass
compensates very readily for being so suddenly
arrested.   If, however, the ground is soft, so as
not of a sudden to arrest the motion of the iceberg, a moraine will be the result; but the
moraine thus raised will tend to bring the iceberg to a stand.   This is the more readily con-
ceived when we contemplate that the power
which impels icebergs is applied to about the
upper third or fourth part of their whole bulk.

The conveying power of icebergs is so well
known to geologists and observers generally that
any remarks I can make here will scarcely add
to their importance, which cannot be too duly
appreciated.   The chief, indeed it may be safely

PHYSICAL GEOGRAPHY, ETC.   179

asserted, the only source from which they receive
foreign matter is the land constituting both sides
of the valleys traversed by the glaciers.   It may,
however, be received from other sources.   I have
often thought that the fragments of a huge iceberg, acquiring a state of quiescence after the
parent mass had separated into such fragments
in one of its fearfully grand revolutions, had
turned up the mud and other earthy matter
from the bottom.   This, however, is doubtful,
for we can hardly conceive it possible that anything extraneous can adhere to hard and brittle
ice passing rapidly through the water.   Icebergs
are sometimes floated so close along a bold and
overhanging rocky coast as to touch the perpen-
dicular cliffs and to remove disintegrated fragments of the rock.   Another, and probably the
most common of these unusual modes is from
coast-ice, which, impelled by the winds and tides,
is often piled up with its load of rounded pebbles,
sand, and mud, against the sides of icebergs.
The foreign matter thus cast upon icebergs must
necessarily be precipitated to the bottom the
first revolution it undergoes; so that it is not
likely to be conveyed to the same distance as
that received by the iceberg while in the form
of a glacier.   In some, cases however, it might

require a few revolutions to cast off the whole of
the adventitious matter received from the coast-
ice.

The quantity of rocky matter which ice is
capable of floating away can be estimated from
the specific gravity of both substances. Taking
2·5 as the specific gravity of granite ·92 as that
of ice, an iceberg, half a mile in breadth, a mile
in length, and two hundred feet in height above
the sea level— dimensions, I may observe, by no
means out of the average—will carry a load of
extraneous matter upwards of one hundred and
fifty millions tons weight. Some of the icebergs seen in Davis Straits are so charged and
impregnated with earthy matter that by an inex-
perienced person they may be mistaken for land
itself. And we often observe large masses of
rock, each upwards of one hundred tons weight,
lying on the surface of the iceberg, or deeply
imbedded in its substance.

By far the greatest number of these floating
worlds, as they may well be termed, dissolve in
Davis Straits, and deposit their earthy contents
throughout its extent. Some of them, however, find their way into the Atlantic, and appear
disposed to push far to the southward into the
temperate zone. As Sir Charles Lyall has

remarked, where the greatest number of these undergo dissolution there the deposition of rocky matter is most active, consisting, as it does, of angular and rounded fragments, together with sand and mud, much of which are from sources of very opposite characters.

Surface ice also is well known as an agent of importance in conveying away to considerable distances the materials of the sea-coast. With strong gales the ice in the Arctic Seas, when free to move in all directions, is driven in upon the coast with great force, and if the bottom about the low water mark is composed of loose gravel or mud, moraines are raised to a height of several feet. The wind ceasing, and high tides proving favourable, the ice again withdraws from the coast, carrying with it large accumulations of the loose shingle or gravel and mud, which it drops in the surrounding sea several hundred miles from their source. The moraines it had raised are not obliterated, and as winter begins to hem the coast with a fringe of ice they cause an irregularity in the surface of the latter by the rise and fall of the tides, which results in a large portion of their contents—pebbles, sand, mud, and probably also abundant traces of animal and vegetable matter—being included in the

new ice formation. This process ceases altogether for that season only with the return of
summer, and then the coast-ice, varying in thickness from two or three up to twenty or more feet
according to the degree of cold and the stillness
of the water, is subject, in some localities at
least, to the power exerted by débâcles in loading it with foreign matter. Thus loaded then it
withdraws from the coast when the straits and
inlets open out and drifts many hundred miles
before it yields itself and its carefully borne
cargo to the sea under the dissolving action of
the sun. We shall find this occurring every
season on the south shore of the North Georgian
Islands. But from the testimony of numerous
travellers, as is shown by Sir Charles Lyall,* it
occurs on a much more magnificent scale at the entrance of the great American and Siberian rivers
which discharge themselves into the Arctic Seas.

The necessity there is for currents into the
Arctic Sea to keep up its mean salinity will
become obvious when we reconsider the vast
amount of fresh water which enters it in the form
of icebergs alone from the heaven descended glaciers. That there are currents out of it is already

---

* Principles of Geology. Seventh Edition. Page 86.

clear enough, otherwise evaporation from its
surface, the greatest part of which is generally
covered with ice, would fail to remove the excess
caused by the annual crop of icebergs, and thus
we should have an icy pile ever growing and
gradually extending into the temperate zone.
The difference of temperature observed on the
two shores of the North Atlantic, amounting as
it does to nearly thirty degrees Fahrenheit's ther-
mometer in lat. 59° during the warmest months
of the year, affords the best possible proof of
the existence of currents in the two directions
that have been indicated. In Davis Straits,
although on a much smaller scale, there is also a
difference in the temperature of the sea on its
two shores. On several occasions during the
late expeditions in search of Sir J. Franklin, and
also previously during Sir W. E. Parry's expedition, while the ships were crossing this strait
from east to west a fall of temperature was
observed. This accounts pretty satisfactorily for
the fact that the east shore during a great part of
the year remains clear of ice while the opposite
is for the most part encumbered; and the greater
mildness of the climate on the east side arises
from the same cause. From the analogy that
appears to exist in point of climate between the

shores of the Atlantic and those of Davis Straits
we may safely infer that in each the causes are
the same, that in the one as well as the other
there is a northerly and a southerly current.

The density of the water assists very mate-
rially in determining the direction of currents in
the Polar seas. By consulting the meteorological abstracts it will be seen how this varied
according to the locality and to the presence or
absence of ice. The apparently greater density
of the sea on the east side of the strait, observed
by all who have yet devoted their attention to
this important subject, is to be assigned to no
other source or cause than a slight northward
movement of the water of the Atlantic into the
strait, and the diminished density on the opposite shore can with equal certainty be assigned
to the constant southward movement of the
diluted and chilly waters of the icy seas. In
the abstracts a few exceptions occur which are
not easily reconciled with these remarks ; they
must be referred to the power exerted by refrigeration and congelation, in precipitating the
saline ingredients of sea-water. Sir W. Edward
Parry found on the west side of Davis Straits,
that the density of the sea came down to $1\cdot018$
when young ice was forming on the surface at a

natural temperature of 30°. And in the abstracts it will be observed almost invariably that the presence of ice diminished the density; and this, in my own estimation, is referable to no cause except the mere effects of refrigeration without congelation or dissolution.

Before, however, this theory of a northerly seeking current into Davis Straits can be finally accepted, we must get over the difficulty arising from the position of the great Arctic current in the North Atlantic. This current we are told sweeps southward across the entrance of Davis Straits, and in this way it must prevent the ingress of any water at the surface from the Atlantic into the Straits. The Rev. Dr. Scoresby, I believe, suggests the idea that two currents varying in temperature may cross by passing the one underneath the other.* The question then arises as to the order of superposition. If sea-water, independent of its saline matter, follows the law of expansion peculiar to water from $+40°$ to $+32°$, one current at a temperature of $+36°$ may rise another at $+44°$, and if we separate the extremes, eight degrees more, the coldest is still the most buoyant, for, even

* Sir Charles Lyall's Principles of Geology, Seventh Edition, p. 79.

although it is sea-water, if in a quiescent state, a portion of it will have become congealed. It is well known that the process of congelation separates the watery from the saline particles. But there seems to me to be no reason why this separation should be confined solely to the act of congelation, since it is owing to the universal law of contraction, observed in obedience to cold by, I believe, everything in nature except water itself, and that only between the temperatures of $+40°$ and $+32°$. This may appear at variance with the experiments of Errman.* Until, however, our knowledge of the physical changes peculiar to these high latitudes extends very considerably, such phenomena as that above alluded to must remain more or less obscure ; at present we may rest assured that a meeting and commingling of waters differing in point of salinity and temperature takes place in the entrance of Davis Straits, and to this, causing sudden and decided changes in the atmosphere, may be attributed in great measure the extreme violence of the storms experienced by navigators when they approach Cape Farewell.

Presuming, then, upon the existence of currents of water from warmer latitudes into the

* Loc. cit. Principles of Geology.

Arctic seas, which may assist the action of the sun in dissolving icebergs and surface ice as well as supply the salts to keep up the mean salinity of these distant ramifications of the ocean, we are in a position to consider the extent and character of deposits and accumulations of " till" now forming in the track of these conveying agents. At the confluence of two opposite currents, the largest amount of foreign matter will be deposited, for these icebergs and coast ice are brought to a stand in the eddies, and are liable to be detained until they dissolve. In such cases submarine ridges and mounds begin to grow above the level of the sea bottom, and they may continue to increase until the surface of the water is reached. A bank in latitude 67° and 68° of the coast of West Greenland, and well known to the whaling and cod-fishing ships by the name Riscoll or Reefkoll, seems to answer this description. The depth of water over the highest part of it does not exceed fifteen fathoms. It appears to be composed of angular fragments of rock, and other materials brought down by icebergs and coast ice. This, however, can only be inferred from the sounding line, and the rough usage to which the lines of the whalers are submitted when they attack and get fast to their prey in its neighbourhood. Its limits can be defined almost at all times by the clusters and groups of small icebergs that ground upon it. And like other banks of a similar character, but of less extent on the same coast, it is exceedingly fertile in shoals of codfish and in abundance of very fine halibut, which frequent it in the months of May, June, July, and August. These and myriads of other fishes including vast numbers of sharks may be found in those seas during the whole year, but this we have not yet had the means of testing so fully as we require. In other parts of Davis Straits and Baffin Bay, where the dredge has been more extensively used, the bottom is composed of fine mud, sand, angular fragments of rock, pebbles, shells, and deposits, resulting from the minute subdivision of calcareous phosphatic and siliceous animal remains, portions of which have been brought up in the dredge from time to time. In the immediate neighbourhood of islands composed of crystalline rocks, the bottom was found to be rocky with occasional plots or patches of accumulations of fragments of the same rock. From a depth of twenty-five to thirty fathoms, at the Hunde Islands, South-east Bay, already noticed, the dredge passed over a loose and softish deposit, and brought up a quantity of dark coloured finely divided matter resembling peat moss, which appeared to have been the result of the decomposition of sea-weed at the bottom ; in some parts the roots, being the hardest and most enduring parts, could be distinguished.

Diatomacea and other minute animal forms, higher in the order of creation, are exceedingly abundant within the Arctic circle. Mud from almost every source has not yet failed to yield considerable varieties, and not a few new species. But the surface-ice undergoing rapid decay by the action of the sun and of the water together, is the source where a person is most successful. It often occurred to me that microscopic forms may be accumulating in a state of great purity, and to a very considerable extent in some of the highly favourable localities so common in Davis Straits. In many of the well sheltered bays where the water is still and the ice dissolves without drifting much about, a brownish slime, consisting of nothing but these forms, in the most perfect and living state, occupies the whole surface of the water among the ice, which after the ice has all disappeared becomes rolled into pellicles by the rippling of the water, and ultimately sinks to the bottom.

This process of deposition, extending over thousands of years, would produce accumulations scarcely second to those of the "berg meal," of Sweden, or of the tripoli of the Isle of France.

In addition to such varied materials as we have indicated, this new formation of "till" will contain abundant remains of animals of a much higher order. Of all parts of the ocean, the polar are those most frequented by the cetacea and the seals. The numbers of the former are very great and that of the latter almost beyond comprehension. In the Greenland seas, especially during the months of March and April, in the vicinity of the island of Jan Mayen, I am informed, that for hundreds of miles the fields of ice are studded with seals, which in the case of the young ones are so tame as to be approached with a "sealing" club, with which they are killed. The bones of these animals must be strewed plentifully on the bottom, and thus they will become constituents of the growing deposit, if they do not undergo decomposition. It may also contain the enduring remains of other mammalia. Every Arctic traveller is aware of the fact, that polar bears are seen on the ice at a great distance to sea, and quite out of sight of land, and my own experience bears testimony to the fact, that not unfrequently they are found swimming in the sea when neither ice nor land is in sight. The Arctic fox, and I believe also the wolf—animals not generally known to take the water, are often set adrift upon the ice and are thus blown out to sea where they perish, when the ice dissolves if they have not previously died of starvation ; and cases are known, although perhaps not recorded, in which human beings have been blown away from the land upon the ice and were never heard of. Two persons of my knowledge have disappeared in this manner from the coast of West Greenland, one of them, however, reached the opposite side of the straits where he spent the remainder of his life, among his less civilized brethren. And the ships engaged in the whaling on the west side of this strait sometimes have to discharge a deed of humanity by taking up from the drifting floes, a group of natives whose avocations had proved too decoying to be safe. So much as allusion has not been made to the remains of reindeer, and the other ruminant inhabitants of these regions, for the reason, that I believe, they frequent the ice much less than the others, and consequently are much less liable to be drifted away ; it is highly probable, however, that their bones sometimes reach the bottom of the Arctic seas, the ice of rivers and inland bays might be the conveying agents. In the event of Davis Straits leaving its bed dry by a subsidence of the sea, or by elevation of the land, we should have to add to our list of natural materials, manufactured articles, such as ships' anchors and cables, broken pottery, and other unimportant, although enduring relics of civilization.

Note.—I cannot allow these remarks to go to press without expressing my regret that time and other circumstances were not sufficiently under control, to enable me to furnish Captain Inglefield with an abstract of the zoological results of our dredgings in Davis Straits. They have been put into the hands of Dr. Gray, of the British Museum, and Prof. E. Forbes, of the Geological Survey, who have kindly undertaken to catalogue those already known, and to describe the new, of which I believe there are several species. If it is not a tribute of respect due to Captain Inglefield, it is at least courtesy to take the liberty of stating here, that no person in the capacity of Commander could have rendered greater assistance and facilities than he did, on every possible occasion, for the advancement of our knowledge of the Natural History of the Arctic Regions.

METEOROLOGY.

ABSTRACTS

OF THE

THREE-HOURLY METEOROLOGICAL REGISTER KEPT ON
BOARD THE DISCOVERY-SHIP "ISABEL,"

BY P. C. SUTHERLAND, ESQ., SURGEON,

IN THE

NORTH ATLANTIC, DAVIS STRAITS, & BAFFIN BAY.

JULY TO NOVEMBER, 1852.

ALSO,

A TABLE

SHEWING

THE INDICATIONS OF THE STANDARD BAROMETER AND
OF TWO ANEROID BAROMETERS, EVERY DAY AT
NOON, DURING THE MONTH OF
SEPTEMBER.

O

METEOROLOGY.

THE following explanations of the abbreviations used in the register, are taken from the "Admiralty Manual of Scientific Inquiry." Instead, however, of using a dot or point underneath any letter, to express an extraordinary degree, I have preferred using an italic, for the purpose of saving space.

Under the heading "Winds," in the column "Estimated Force," numbers from 1 to 12 denote the force of the wind; thus,—0, denotes *calm;* 1, *light air,* just perceptible; 2, *light breeze,* in which a ship, clean full, in smooth water, would go from one to two knots; 3, *gentle breeze* (from two to four knots); 4, *moderate breeze* (from four to six knots); 5, *fresh breeze,* in which a ship *could just carry,* on a wind, royals, &c.; 6, *stormy breeze* (single-reefed topsails and top-gallant sails); 7, *moderate gale* (double-reefed, &c.); 8, *fresh gale* (triple-reefed and courses); 9, *stormy gale,* (close-reefed, &c.); 10, *whole gale* (close-reefed main-topsail, and reefed foresail); 11, *storm* (storm staysails); 12, *hurricane* (no canvass can stand).

Under the heading "Weather," b. denotes *blue sky,* be the atmosphere clear or heavy; c. *clouds,* detached opening clouds; d. *drizzling rain;* f. *foggy;* g. *gloomy,* dark weather; h. *hail;* l. *lightning;* m. *misty,* hazy atmosphere; o. *overcast,* the whole sky covered with thick clouds; p. *passing* temporary showers; q. *squally;* r. *rain,* continued rain; s. *snow;* t. *thunder;* u. *ugly*

o 2

threatening appearance; v. *visibility of objects,* clear atmosphere; w. *wet.* (dew.)

And under the heading " Clouds according to Howard's nomenclature," c. *cirrus,* expresses a cloud resembling a lock of hair or a feather, consisting of streaks, wisps, and fibres, and vulgarly known as mares' tails; κ. *cumulus,* denotes a cloud in dense convex heaps, or rounded forms definitely terminated above, indicating saturation of the upper clear region of the air, and a rising supply of vapour from below; s. *stratus,* in an extended continuous level sheet, which must not be confounded with the flat base of the *cumulus,* when it simply reposes on the vapour plain; n. *nimbus,* is a dense cloud, spreading out into a crown of *cirrus* above, and passing beneath into a shower. The combinations κs., cs., and cκ., denoting *cumulo-stratus, cirro-stratus,* and *cirro-cumulus,* are sufficiently plain without any explanation.

METEOROLOGICAL TABLES.

ABSTRACT OF THE METEOROLOGICAL JOURNAL KEPT ON BOARD THE DISCOVERY SHIP ISABEL, CAPT. INGLEFIELD, R.N., JULY, 1852.—*North Atlantic.*

Dates.	Standard Barometer, corrected for capillary action, and reduced to 32° of Fahrenheit.			Reading of the Thermometer in the Shade at								Mean Daily Temperature.	Sea Water at Surface.	
	Max.	Min.	Mean.	3 A.M.	6 A.M.	9 A.M.	Noon	3 P.M.	6 P.M.	9 P.M.	Mid-night		Mean Daily Tem.	Density at 60° Fahr.
	In.	In.	In.	°	°	°	°	°	°	°	°	°	°	°
12	30·11	30·10	30·10					59	60	59	55	58·1	53·5	1·0275
*13	30·03	29·96	30·01				60	65	65	63	60	62·6	56·3	1·0275
14	29·97	·87	29·93				62	63	63	63	61	62·4	57	1·0275
†15	·78	·76	·78				61	63	63	63	61	62·2	56·3	1·0275
16	·80	·76	·80			63	61	60	61	60	56	60·1	55·5	1·0275
17	·79	·60	·68			60	61	60	60	53	55	58·1	55·7	1·0275
18	·59	·49	·54	55	56	57	57	57	57	56	56	56·4	56	1·027
§19	·69	·61	·63	55	56	57	57	56	58	56	55	56·2	56	1·027
20	·71	·64	·67	55	56	63	64	65	58	57	57	59·4	57·2	1·026
21	·67	·58	·65	54	55	56	57	57	56	53	53	55·1	57	1·027
22	·67	·50	·58	53	53	53	54	57	55	53	55	58·1	53·6	1·027
‡23	·42	·28	·33	53	53	54	55	54	53	50	50	52·3	53·7	1·027
24	·71	·35	·53	50	50	55	54	59	54	52	52	53·2	55	1·027
25	·90	·73	·83	50	52	53	57	57	51	50	40	51·2	55	1·027
26	·92	·76	·87	48	48	48	53	55	53	53	53	51·4	54·5	1·026
27	·82	·69	·71	53	54	55	55	54	53	53	51	53·6	53	1·027
**28	·90	·79	·87	50	50	54	57	55	53	53	50	53·0	51·1	1·026
29	·79	·59	·64	49	49	50	51	48	49	49	50	49·9	49	1 026
30	·70	·60	·65	44	45	45	47	47	47	45	38	44·7	45	1·026
31	·69	·64	·67	37	37	38	38	39	40	36	34	37·4	33·9	1·023
Means														

* *Medusæ* and *Gammarinæ* abundant.

† *Anatifa* of large size, floating in the surface in great abundance; a small *decapodous* crustacean, and *Gammarinæ*, also abundant.

‡ Porpoises in playful 'schools.' Sea not luminous, but containing *Cetochilidæ* and brownish *Medusæ*, and also sea-jelly (*Thalassicolla*).

§ *Anomalocera Patersonii*, and other *Entomostraca*, in great numbers, in the surface; Rorquaal whales, and porpoises.

** *Procellaria capensis* seen.

ABSTRACT OF THE METEOROLOGICAL JOURNAL KEPT ON BOARD THE DISCOVERY
SHIP ISABEL, CAPT. INGLEFIELD, R.N., JULY, 1852.—*North Atlantic.*

Dates.	WINDS.		WEATHER.		Clouds, according to Howard's nomenclature.	Position at Noon.		
	Direction.	Estimated Force.	A.M.	P.M.		Lat.	Long.	Names of Places.
						° ′	° ′	
12	SOUTHERLY.	3–4	v.b.c. : d.o.m.		C.K.	...	...	In the Roost.
13	S.S.E.	3–1	v.b.c. : v.b.c.		CK.K.	59 43	4 8	
14	VARIABLE.	0–1	v.o.c.		CK.K.	59 46	5 42	N. Atlantic.
*15	S., VARIABLE.	2–1	v.b.o.c. : m.f.		K.	59 49	7 49	
16	S.S.W., VBLE.	1–2	f.		...	60 14	9 25	
†17	S.E.	3	v.o.c. : f.m.		...	59 54	12 41	
18	W.N.W.	3	v.o.c.		K.N.	59 32	14 41	
19	S.S.W.	6–4	v.b.o.c.r.q.		N.K.	59 11	16 57	
20	S.E.	5–2	v.b.c.r.		S.CK.	58 4	19 55	
21	N.W.	4–7	v.b.c.		K.	58 11	21 11	
22	N.W. to S.W.	7–6	v.b c.r. : q.b.c.		K.N.	58 59	23 14	
23	S.W., VBLE.	3–2	v.b.c. : q.p.r.		K.N.	60 14	25 45	
24	VBLE., N.W.	4–3	v.b.r. : v.b.c.		K.N.	60 35	27 50	
25	W. to N.W.	3–5	v.b.c. : v.b.c.p.q.		K.N.	60 35	26 23	
26	N.W. to S.E.	0–4	v.b.c.p.q. : v.o.c.		K.	59 58	29 1	
27	S.E. to N.E.	4–5	o.f.r.d. : m.o.c.d.		K.	59 49	32 41	
‡28	N.E. to S.E.	4–5	v.b.c. : v.o.c.		CS.CK.	59 23	36 43	
29	E.S.E.	4–5	m.d.r.o.		....	58 59	40 31	
§30	E.S.E.	5–4	m.d.r.o. : v.b.c.		CS.K.	58 52	43 17	Cape Farewell.
**31	S.E., VBLE.	3–1	o.c.m. : v.c.m.		N.CK.	59 57	46 6	Davis Straits.
Means								

* The temperature in the cabins, when the furnace is lighted, varies from 70° up to nearly 100°.

† Standard barometer transferred to the small cabin, where it is placed at an elevation of about two feet above the sea-level.

‡ Fine clear weather. Aurora Borealis of a golden-yellow colour, extending in distinct coruscations to near the zenith, from an irregularly defined arch on the northern sky. Temperature of sea and density diminishing as the west side of the Atlantic is reached, owing doubtless to the almost constant presence of ice drifting from high northern latitudes.

§ Saw some icebergs at Cape Farewell.

** Came in among drifting ice.

ABSTRACT OF THE METEOROLOGICAL JOURNAL KEPT ON BOARD THE DISCOVERY SHIP ISABEL, CAPT. INGLEFIELD, R.N., AUGUST, 1852.—*Davis Straits, &c.*

Dates.	Standard Barometer, corrected for capillary action, and reduced to 32° Fahrenheit.			Reading of the Thermometer in the Shade at								Mean Daily Temperature.	Sea Water at Surface.	
	Max.	Min.	Mean.	3 A.M.	6 A.M.	9 A.M.	Noon	3 P.M.	6 P.M.	9 P.M.	Mid-night		Mean Daily Tem.	Density at 60° Fahr.
	In.	In.	In.	°	°	°	°	°	°	°	°	°	°	
1	29·86	29·69	29·79	33	33	35	36	43	43	42	45	38·4	39·6	1·024
2	94	·80	·89	37	37	36	40	40	40	42	44	39·5	44	1·025
*3	30·01	·91	·95	44	44	45	45	45	43	43	40	43	43	1·025
4	29·96	·60	·78	38	36	34	38	44	40	39	37	38·2	36·1	1·025
5	60	·48	·53	36	37	38	39	39	38	40	38	38·1	38·2	1·025
6	·65	·62	·63	37	37	37	40	42	40	38	38	38·6	38	1·024
7	·73	·58	·63	39	42	42	40	43	42	40	40	41	38·7	1·024
8	·83	·75	·78	38	40	44	43	41	40	39	36	40·1	38·7	1·023
9	·91	·75	·87	38	44	43	43	40	30	40	40	39·7	38·7	1·024
10	·86	·74	·79	40	40	40	40	40	40	40	40	40	40	1·024
11	·87	·69	·78	40	39	41	43	42	41	41	40	40·8	39·5	1·025
12	·73	·69	·72	40	40	41	42	41	41	40	40	40·6	40	1·024
†13	·79	·64	·78	40	39	38	40	41	39	36	36	38·9	39·4	1·023
14	·75	·64	·74	37	38	39	40	40	40	39	38	38·8	38·1	1·023
15	·58	·34	·51	37	39	42	43	44	43	40	38	40·7	39·4	1·024
16	·43	·20	·30	36	37	39	43	40	40	38	36	38·6	37·5	1·025
17	·51	·41	·45	36	37	40	43	42	47	38	36	40	36·4	1·0235
18	·40	·54	46	36	36	36	38	39	38	36	37	37	37·2	1·0235
‡19	·40	·47	·43	36	35	33	34	34	33	32	32	33·6	35·6	1·0235
20	43	·64	·51	31	30	31	31	32	32	31	32	31·2	32	1·023
§21	·71	·61	·67	31	31	32	34	34	33	30	28	31·6	30·5	1·020
**22	56	·46	·52	28	28	29	30	30	34	30	28	29·7	30·8	1·022
23	·44	·29	·39	29	28	33	33	34	33	33	32	31·9	31	1·023
24	·29	·13	·19	32	32	33	37	36	36	34	33	34·1	32	1·023
††25	·82	·26	·55	32	32	32	35	35	33	32	32	32·9	32	1·023
26	·84	·73	·76	32	33	34	34	34	34	34	34	33·6	32·6	1·0235
‡‡27	·73	·29	·49	34	33	32	30	25	26	27	27	29·3	28·7	1·0235
28	·75	·28	·56	28	29	30	30	27	28	28	30	29·8	30	1·023
29	·82	·72	·78	29	30	32	32	30	30	30	28	30·1	30	1·0235
30	·70	·59	·64	25	26	28	30	33	30	30	30	29	30·4	1·0235
31	·79	·74	·76	28	27	29	30	30	30	28	27	28·6	30·4	1·0235
Means														

* *Thalassicolla* thickening the water (at the surface only); *Cetochilus arcticus* exceedingly abundant a few feet beneath the surface.

† Fulmars and kittiwakes in immense numbers, in North-east Bay,—a favourite breeding-place for these birds.

‡ *Clio helicina* and *borealis, Cetochilus articus,* an *Amphipodous* crustacean, *Sagitta bipunctata,* and hosts of *Medusæ,* in the surface.

§ *Acidians,* from muddy bottom, at a depth of fifty fathoms.

** *Chroditæ, Annelides, Brittle Stars,* and *Isopodous* crustaceans, from muddy bottom, twenty-five fathoms.

†† Sea abundant in drifting seaweed and *Entomostraca* of very large size.

‡‡ Water rather abundant in *Sagitta* and *Cetochilus,* at Cape Alexander and in Smith Sound.

ABSTRACT OF THE METEOROLOGICAL JOURNAL KEPT ON BOARD THE DISCOVERY SHIP ISABEL, CAPT. INGLEFIELD, R.N., AUGUST, 1852.—*Davis Straits.*

Dates.	WINDS.		WEATHER.		Clouds, according to Howard's nomenclature.	Position at Noon.		
	Direction.	Estimated Force.	A.M.	P.M.		Lat.	Long.	Names of Places.
1	N.W.	0–5	v.c.o.f. : m.o.c.		N.K.	60 0	48 30	Cape Farewell.
*2	N.N.W.	2–5	v.b.		C.S.	60 10	49 40	Davis Straits, E.
3	N.W.	5–4	v.b.f. : b.v.c.		C.K.	60 21	49 36	[shore.
4	N.W.	4–3	v.b.c.		CK.S.	61 4	49 50	
†5	N.W.	2–6	f. : m.o.c.		K.N.S.	62 6	50 58	
6	N.W., VBLE.	4–1	v.b.c.		CS.K.	62 11	52 30	Cape Desolation.
7	N.W.	5–6	v.b.		CS.	63 5	51 50	Lichtenfels.
8	N.W. to S.W.	0–5	v.b.c.		CS.K.	63 7	51 15	Fiskernaes.
9	S.S.E.	2–7	v.b.c. : r.m.c.o.		CS.K.	63 40	53 0	Godhaab.
10	S.S.E.	7	r.m.c.o.		K.N.	66 0	54 0	Sukkertoppen.
11	S.E. to N.E.	6–0	r.m.c.o. : v.b.c.		S.CK.	68 3	55 10	Off Riscoll.
12	S.E. to N.E.	0–1	m.c.o. : r.m.c.o.		...	69 4	53 50	Godhavn.
‡13	S.W.	1–4	r.m.c.o. : v.b.c.o.		N.K.	70 15	55 30	Off Disco Island.
14	S.E.	3–1	v.b.c. : v.b.c.o.		K.CS.	71 26	56 20	Black Hook.
15	N.E.	0–2	v.b.c.		CK.CS.	72 32	56 40	Proven.
16	N.E. to S.W.	1–6	v.b.c. : o.c.m.		CK.S.	72 50	56 10	Uppernivik.
17	N.N.W.	0–2	v.b.c. : f.		CS.K.	73 20	57 26	Berry Island.
§18	S.E. to S.W.	4–1	o.m.c.r. : o.c.b.v.		N.CS	74 10	58 40	Melville Bay.
19	W. to N.E.	1–0	v.b.c.m. : m.o.c.		K.CK.	75 20	60 0	Melville Bay.
**20	S.W.	1–3	v.b.o.c. : v.b.c.m.		N.CK.	75 25	65 10	Melville Bay.
††21	S.E. to N.	0–4	v.b.c.m. : v.b.c.		K.N.CK.	75 52	67 30	Cape York.
22	NORTH.	4–3	v.b.c.		CK. CS.	76 20	70 5	C. Dudley Diggs.
23	N.E. to S W.	3–1	v.b.c. : p.m.o.c.		CS.K.	76 34	69 30	Wolstenholme Snd.
24	N.W. to S.W.	1–4	v.m.o.c. : v.b.c.		CK.C.	76 45	71 0	Booth Sound.
‡‡25	N.W. to S.E.	6–4	v.b.c : v.o.c.		CK.S.	77 5	71 45	Whale Sound.
26	S.E. to N.W.	3–1	v.b.o.c.		K.C.CK.	77 30	76 0	Cape Saumarez.
27	N.W. to N.E.	3–10	v.b.c.		N.K.	78 28	75 40	Smith Sound.
§§28	N.E. to S.W.	10–2	o.m.p.s.r.		...	77 50	77 30	Top Baffin Bay.
29	S.E. to N.W.	1–2	m.o.c. : v.b.o.c.		K.CK.S.	77 30	76 0	Cape Isabella.
30	N.W. to S.W.	2–3	v.b.c.		CK.S.	76 51	76 30	Cape Mowat.
31	S.W. to W.	4–2	v.b.o.c m.		K.CK.S.	76 10	80 30	Jones' Sound.
Means								

* A good deal of ice encountered off Capes Farewell and Desolation. Aurora in yellow and reddish coruscations on the western sky, extending near the zenith.
† Icebergs abundant on the coast. Temperature and density of sea increase as we leave the coast for the middle of the Strait.
‡ The land is quite black at and a little above the sea-level, but higher up it is covered with recently fallen snow.
§ Icebergs most abundant; often heard crumbling to pieces.
** Among ice.
†† One hundred and eighty icebergs, on a semicircle of twelve miles.
‡‡ Large extent of open water; very few icebergs.
§§ East shore not so much enveloped in ice and snow as the west side of Baffin Bay; drifting, and in some cases fixed ice, along the west coast.

ABSTRACT OF THE METEOROLOGICAL JOURNAL KEPT ON BOARD THE DISCOVERY SHIP ISABEL, CAPT. INGLEFIELD, R.N., SEPTEMBER, 1852.—*Davis Straits, &c.*

Dates.	Standard Barometer, corrected for capillary action, and reduced to 32° Fahrenheit.			Reading of the Thermometer in the Shade at								Mean Daily Temperature.	Sea Water at Surface.	
	Max.	Min.	Mean.	3 A.M.	6 A.M.	9 A.M.	Noon	3 P.M.	6 P.M.	9 P.M.	Midnight		Mean Daily Tem.	Density at 60° Fahr.
	In.	In.	In.	°	°	°	°	°	°	°	°	°	°	
*1	29·73	29·45	29·55	28	27	28	28	28	27	27	28	27·6	29·6	1·0235
2	·58	·45	·51	28	28	29	29	29	29	26	25	28	29·5	1·022
3	·74	·62	·69	24	28	29	32	31	28	28	28	28·5	30	1·024
4	·74	·62	·71	27	28	28	29	30	30	25	26	27·9	30·5	1·024
5	·63	·58	·60	24	25	26	25	25	24	24	24	24·6	29·1	1·0245
6	·63	·55	·58	23	24	24	25	24	24	24	22	23·7	29	1·0235
7	·86	·65	·73	22	23	24	27	27	26	24	21	24·7	28·4	1·024
8	30·02	·89	·97	22	25	28	29	29	25	24	24	25·8	29	1·0235
9	29·97	·77	·84	25	28	29	29	26	26	25	24	26·5	29	1·0235
10	·96	·78	·85	24	24	25	26	26	23	22	22	24	29	1·024
11	30·19	30·02	30·12	21	22	25	25	26	26	26	26	24·4	29·6	1·024
12	·20	29·11	·13	26	26	27	27	28	28	28	28	27·2	30	1·024
13	29·98	·88	29·94	27	28	26	29	29	26	27	26	27·3	30	1·024
14	·98	·56	·79	28	30	30	30	27	28	28	28	28·6	30	1·0235
†15	·98	·57	·73	27	27	30	29	30	30	30	29	29	30	1·0235
16	30·28	30·05	30·20	28	29	30	32	31	29	30	30	29·8	30	1·024
17	·29	29·95	·15	30	30	30	30	30	29	28	25	29	30	1·024
18	29·85	·84	29·87	24	24	26	27	27	31	31	30	27·5	31·5	1·0235
19	·87	·74	·80	29	29	30	30	30	25	24	24	27·3	32·5	1·023
20	·74	·64	·67	24	25	26	26	26	25	25	27	25·5	31	1·023
‡21	·77	·71	·75	25	24	26	26	26	26	26	25	25·6	30	1·023
22	·83	·79	·81	26	26	26	30	31	30	28	28	28·1	31·5	1·023
23	·98	·87	·92	28	28	28	29	31	30	30	30	29·2	32	1·0235
24	·82	·28	·60	30	31	32	32	32	32	32	32	31·6	32	1·0235
25	·90	·18	·47	32	32	32	32	31	31	32	34	32	32·1	1·024
26	30·03	·81	·95	34	34	35	34	35	37	37	38	35·5	33·6	1·024
27	·79	·68	·76	38	38	38	38	38	39	39	39	38·6	34	1·024
28	·84	·61	·68	39	39	39	38	38	38	38	35	38	34	1·024
29	30·16	·96	30·02	35	34	32	34	34	34	34	32	33·6	33·1	1·024
30	·21	30·04	·12	31	32	32	32	32	31	30	30	31·2	33·5	1·0245
Means														

* *Clio helicina* almost the only creature found in the water; hardly any *Algæ.*

† *Bivalves* and *Gasteropods*, together with *Radiata* and *Crustaceans*, (*Saduria, Idotea, Crangon,* &c.,) occur at the muddy bottom, 12 to 18 fathoms; *Chroditæ* also found; *Algæ* extremely rare. Molleymokes and loons occuring, but not abundant; rotgés often seen at the 'middle ice.'

‡ Ivory gulls abundant at the 'middle ice,' but rarely coming to either side of the Straits.

ABSTRACT OF THE METEOROLOGICAL JOURNAL KEPT ON BOARD THE DISCOVERY SHIP ISABEL, CAPT. INGLEFIELD, R.N., SEPTEMBER, 1852.—*Davis Straits, &c.*

Dates.	WINDS.			WEATHER.		Clouds, according to Howard's nomenclature.	Position at Noon.			
	Direction.	Estimated Force.		A.M.	P.M.		Lat.		Long.		Names of Places.
							° ′	° ′		
*1	W.N.W.	5–6		q.m.o.c.s.p.		K.N.	76 11	85 20		Jones' Sound.
2	S.S.W.	3–4		p.s.o. : *v.b.c.*		CK.S.	75 9	78 0		Cape Fitzroy.
3	N.W.	0–2		*v.b* c.		CK.S.	74 30	82 0		Cape Warrender.
4	S.E. to N.W.	1–3		v.b.c.o.		K.N.	74 30	83 10		Croker Bay.
5	N.W.	3–5		v.b c.		K.	74 24	85 30		Powell Inlet.
6	N.W.	3–1		v.b.c.		KS.K.	74 30	86 45		Maxwell Bay.
†7	E S.E.	1–5		m.o.c.s. : v.b.c.		CK.K.S.	74 43	92 0		Beechey Island.
8	E.N E	5–7		*v.b.c.* : v.b.c.		K.OS.	74 20	90 40		Radstock Bay.
‡9	E.N.E to N.W.	7–3		v.b.c.		K.OS.	74 20	88 40		Maxwell Bay.
10	N.W. to W.	2–4		v.b.c. : v.o.c.		CK.S.	73 58	83 45		Croker Bay.
11	W. to S.	4–1		v.s.p. : v.b.c.		CK.N.	74 8	81 20		Navy Board Inlet.
§12	S. to S.E.	1–6		v.b.c. : q.r.s.p.q.		CK.N.	73 55	78 30		Cape Hay.
13	S.E. to N.	6–1		o.s. : m.o.s.c.		N.K.	73 39	76 45		Cape W. Bathurst.
14	N. to S.E	1–3		v.b.o.c. : g.o.s.		KS.N.	72 30	75 30		Cape Bowen.
15	N. to N.W.	1–3		o.s. : *o.s.v.*		KS.	71 25	72 30		Cape Adair.
16	N. and S.E.	1–4		v.b.c. : v.o.c.		OS.CK.	71 5	70 0		Scott Inlet.
17	S.S.E.	7–4		g.v.o.c. : v.b.c.		K.	71 0	69 0		Agnes Monument.
18	S.E. and N.W.	4–1–3		*v.b.c.*		KS.	71 12	69 0		"Middle Ice."
19	N.W. and S E.	2–9	v.o.c.p.s. : *o.s.q.*			K.	71 25	68 0		In Davis Straits.
20	N.W.	9–4		g.v.b.c.p.s.		K.KS.	71 12	65 21		"Middle Ice."
**21	N.W. and S.E.	3–3		v.b.o c.		⸵KS.K.	71 20	62 28		"Middle Ice."
22	NORTH.	4–6		*v.b.c.* : v.o.c.		O.KS.	71 12	61 30		"Middle Ice."
23	W. to S.E.	5–9		v.o.c. : *v.b.c.*		CK.S.	69 41	61 30		"East Water" of
24	S.E.	9–11		v.b.c. : *o.s.*		K.	69 0	62 8	⎰ Davis Straits.
25	S.E. to W.	10–8		o.s.p.v.		K.S.	70 0	58 0		"East Water."
26	S.S.E.	10–6		r.p.q. : v.b.c.		K.OS.	70 15	57 6		Disco Island.
27	S.S.E.	11–8		o.r.q. : v.o.c.		K.	70 25	59 0		"East Water" of
28	S.S.E.	11–9		o.c.r.q.		...	70 30	58 20	⎰ Davis Straits.
††29	S.S.E., VBLE.	6–1		v.b.c. : o.c.		K.CK.	70 46	58 0		Disco Island.
30	N. to W.	1–2		v.b.c. : v.b.o.c.		K.	70 36	58 0		Off Disco Island.
Means										

* The surface ice of great thickness (25 to 30 feet), in Jones Sound; a few small icebergs met.

† Land around Beechy Island covered with snow; ice forming in Erebus and Terror Bay.

‡ Hardly any ice in Lancaster Sound.

§ Loose ice off Cape Byam Martin; icebergs numerous. Nights dark and long.

** Young ice forming of considerable thickness among the floes of the old ice in the middle of the Straits.

†† Temperature and density of sea increased as we approach the east side of the Straits. It has blown an exceedingly violent and most protracted gale; heavy sea; very few icebergs.

ABSTRACT OF THE METEOROLOGICAL JOURNAL KEPT ON BOARD THE DISCOVERY SHIP ISABEL, CAPT. INGLEFIELD, R.N., OCTOBER, 1852.—*Davis Straits.*

Dates.	Standard Barometer, corrected for capillary action, and reduced to 32° Fahrenheit.			Reading of the Thermometer in the Shade at								Mean Daily Temperature.	Sea Water at Surface.	
	Max.	Min.	Mean.	3 A.M.	6 A.M.	9 A.M.	Noon	3 P.M.	6 P.M.	9 P.M.	Midnight		Mean Daily Tem.	Density at 60° Fahr.
	In.	In.	In.	°	°	°	°	°	°	°	°	°	°	
1	30·35	30·21	30·26	29	31	36	36	36	36	35	33	34·2	36·6	1·0245
2	·41	·34	·38	32	35	37	40	43	32	30	30	34·8	36·6	1·0245
3	·33	29·97	·32	30	32	35	36	33	34	35	36	34	35·7	1·0245
4	29·99	·89	29·92	35	35	37	38	36	36	37	37	36·4	36	1·0245
*5	·91	·78	·81	37	39	39	40	41	40	39	38	39·1	36·9	1·0245
6	·80	·66	·76	34	31	32	35	36	35	35	35	34·1	35·1	1·024
7	·61	·40	·48	35	35	36	36	39	38	39	39	37·1	35·2	1·024
8	·73	·55	·69	38	38	38	37	36	35	34	33	36·1	35	1·024
9	·90	·74	·82	33	33	33	33	32	32	33	33	32·8	35	1·024
10	30·25	·92	30·07	32	32	31	32	30	29	28	28	30·2	35	1·024
†11	·21	·94	·02	28	29	32	33	33	30	30	30	30·6	33·3	1·0235
12	29·92	·61	29·77	29	28	28	28	28	27	27	28	27·9	30·2	1·0235
13	·61	·45	·55	31	32	33	34	33	33	34	33	32·8	33·1	1·025
14	·72	·40	·51	33	33	32	33	32	32	32	32	32·3	34·1	1·025
15	·88	·75	·81	33	34	35	38	36	36	36	35	35·4	39·2	1·0255
16	·88	·34	·65	36	36	38	37	37	35	34	35	36	39·6	1·025
17	·31	·12	·19	36	40	40	41	40	38	37	36	38·5	41	1·0255
18	·78	·46	·67	36	34	33	36	34	33	33	33	34·4	40·7	1·0255
19	·91	·82	·87	33	33	34	35	36	34	35	34	34·2	41·1	1·026
20	·89	·78	·82	34	33	34	38	38	38	38	37	36·4	41·6	1·0265
21	·91	·80	·84	38	39	41	39	41	39	39	42	38·5	43·6	1·0265
‡22	·87	·79	·86	42	42	42	42	44	43	43	43	42·6	46·6	1·0265
23	·77	·66	·72	43	43	46	44	44	44	44	44	44	47·9	1·0265
24	·77	·55	·70	44	44	45	45	45	44	40	40	43·3	48·7	1·026
25	·69	·44	·57	40	39	39	42	41	43	45	46	41·9	49·1	1·0265
26	80	·70	·71	48	49	50	50	49	45	49	46	48·2	51·2	1·0265
27	·82	·72	·77	46	48	48	52	51	47	51	50	49·3	51·6	1·0265
28	·79	·62	·70	49	49	49	50	52	52	52	50	50·4	53	1·0265
29	·61	·43	·47	49	46	46	46	47	47	47	46	46·7	52·7	1·0265
30	·43	·14	·30	46	47	47	48	48	47	48	47	47·2	51·7	1·0265
31	·12	28·80	29·00	47	48	48	49	49	49	49	49	48·5	51·2	1·0265
Means														

* At every depth, from 2 to 100 fathoms, *Crustacea, Mollusca, Annelides, Echinoderms* (Brittle Stars, &c.), *Flustræ, Sertulariæ* and other corals, occur in the utmost profusion in the vicinity of the Hunde Islands, although the bottom is much subjected to iceberg action. Large heaps of seaweed are thrown up on the beach here, as in Whale Sound.

† Myriads of eider-ducks, young and old, in the middle of the Straits.

‡ Loons, sea-parrots, and fulmars, abundant; snow-buntings attempting to alight on board.

Abstract of the Meteorological Journal kept on board the Discovery Ship Isabel, Capt. Inglefield, R.N., October, 1852.—*Davis Straits.*

Dates.	Winds.		Weather		Clouds, according to Howard's nomenclature.	Position at Noon.		
	Direction.	Estimated Force.	A.M.	P.M.		Lat.	Long.	Names of Places.
*1	N.E. to N.W.	8–1	v.b.c.q. : v.b.c.		cs.ck.	69 22	54	Off Disco Island.
2	s. to N.E.	1–2	v.b.c. : v.b.c.		cs.k.	68 50	53 30	South-east Bay.
3	E.N.E.	3–9	v.b. : v.b.		cs.c.	68 52	53 29	Hunde Islands.
4	E.N.E. to S.E.	8–5–9	v.b. : v.o.r.		cs.cn.	68 52	53 29	
5	s. to s.w.	9–3	o.r.d.m.		cs.	68 52	53 29	
†6	s.w. to s.e.	4–5	v.b.c.		ck.	68 52	53 29	
7	s.e. to s.w.	9–11	v.d.r.g.m.		k.n.	68 52	53 40	South-east Bay.
8	s.w. to s.	10–3	v.b.c.q.p.		ks.k.	69 15	57	Davis Straits.
9	s.s.w.	2–6	v.b.c.s. : v.b.c.q.		ks.	69 23	57 41	"East Water."
10	s.w. to N.	2–5–1	v.b.c.q. : v.b.c.		k.ks.	68 30	55 10	Off Riscoll.
11	N.E.	3–9	v.b.c. : v.b.c.q.p.		k.n.	67 34	58	Crossing Davis
‡12	N.N.E.	10–11	v.b.c.q.p.r.s.o.		k.n.	66 34	60 50	Straits to west side.
13	VARIABLE, E.	8–2	o.m.d.r. : v.b.c.		o.k.	64 7	60 57	In the entrance of
14	VARIABLE, S.W.	4–7	v.b.c.q.p.r.s.		c.k.n.	63 39	60 41	Davis Straits.
15	VARIABLE, S.W.	7–5	v.b.c.q.p.r.s		ck.cs.	62 29	57 39	
16	s.w. to E.	2–9	v.b.c. : v.b.c.q.		os.k.	61 40	56 29	In the lower parts
17	E. to N.W.	9–2–9	o.s.p.r.g.v.h.		n.k.c.	60 41	55 30	of Davis Straits.
18	N.W.	9–7–9	v.b.c.q.p.s.h.		k.cs.n.	59 21	53 39	
19	N.W.	8–6	v.b.c.q.p.s.h.		k.cs.n.	57 27	50 21	
20	N.N.W.	6–8	v.b.c.p.s.h.		n.k.	56 4	47 41	Off Cape Farewell.
§21	W.N.W.	8–7	v.b.c.q.p.h.r.		n.k.	56 17	42 51	
22	N.W.	5–4	v.b.c.q.p.r.		n.k.c.	55 58	39 7	Crossing the Atlantic.
23	N.W.	6–5	v.b.c.p.r.		n.k.	55 54	35 36	
24	W.N.W.	6–7	v.b.c.p.r.o.		n.k.	56 6	31 26	
25	W.N.W.	9–7	v.b.c.r.p.q.		k.n.	57	27 30	
26	N.N.E.	9–4	r.p.q. : v.b.c.		k.n.	57 24	23 13	
27	E.S.E.	4–5	v.b.c.		k.s.c.	57 23	21 46	
28	E.	5–6	v.b.c. : v.b.c.		k.s.	57 34	21 27	
29	E.S.E.	7–10	v.o.c.r.p.q.		k.n.	59 3	21 20	
30	E.S.E.	9–10	v.b.c.r.p.q.		k.n.	59 56	21 20	
**31	E.N.E.	10–7	v.o.c.r.p.		k.c.n.	59 20	20 37	
Means								

* The land, quite black and free from snow, along the east coast of Davis Straits, beneath an elevation of 1000 feet.

† The surface of the land frozen at the sea-level; pools on it have one to two inches thickness of ice on their surface.

‡ Density and temperature of the sea decrease, as the west side of the Straits is approached.

§ Weather exceedingly disturbed. Aurora Borealis frequently most brilliant.

** Towards the end of this month easterly winds have prevailed to an unusual extent.

ABSTRACT OF THE METEOROLOGICAL JOURNAL KEPT ON BOARD THE DISCOVERY SHIP ISABEL, CAPT. INGLEFIELD, R.N., NOVEMBER, 1852.—*North Atlantic.*

Dates.	Standard Barometer, corrected for capillary action, and reduced to 32° Fahrenheit.			Reading of the Thermometer in the Shade at								Mean Daily Temperature.	Sea Water at Surface.	
	Max.	Min.	Mean.	3 A.M.	6 A.M.	9 A.M.	Noon	3 P.M.	6 P.M.	9 P.M.	Mid-night		Mean Daily Tem.	Density at 60° Fahr.
	In.	In.	In.	°	°	°	°	°	°	°	°	°	°	
1	28·78	28·54	28·63	49	49	49	50	50	49	49	48	49·1	52	1·0265
2	29·12	·83	29·06	47	47	47	46	47	47	47	46	46·7	51·2	1·0265
3	·23	29·13	·21	46	48	50	49	48	48	48	48	48·1	52	1·0265
4	·62	·34	·48	48	48	50	51	50	48	49	49	49·1	52·5	1·027
5	·61	·03	·35	49	49	50	50	50	50	50	50	49·7	52·6	1·027
6	·35	·05	·22	50	50	47	50	51	50	47	46	49·2	51·4	1·0225
7	·31	·09	·16	46	45	47	51	52	53	54	54	50·2	48	1·027
8	·85	·23	·50	50	48	46	48	46	45	43	49	47·5	48·5	1 027
9	30·06	·90	·96	38	36	38	38	42	41	41	40	38·9	49	1·027
10	·04	·92	·99	40	40	43	44	43	41	42	42	41·9	50·1	1·027
11	29·86	·64	·74	43	42	40	40	42	44	44	42	42·1	51	1·027
12	·83	·73	·80	42	41	42	43	42	42	41	42	41·9	48·4	1·025
13	·79	·53	·63	41	40	40	41	40	40	39	39	40	47	1·0255
14	·52	·38	·45	39	38	39	39	39	38	39	39	38·7	46·6	1·026
15	·33	·03	·17	39	40	40	41	42	43	44	44	41·6	45·2	1·0225
16	28·98	28·80	28·88	44	44	44	45	45	45	45	43	44·4	45·5	1·0235
17	·93	·89	·90	44	44	44	48	45	43	43	43	44·2	44·3	1·0175
18	29·46	·84	29·14	45	43	44	48	46	46	43	44	44·9	47·4	1·0255
19	.67	29·51	·57	43	43	43	48	47	48	49	49	46·2	50·3	1·026
20	·51	·27	·37	47	47	49	50	50	51	52	49	49·3	49·7	1·0255
21	·25	·08	·15	49	47	51	51	51	52	52	52	50·6	50·1	1·0255
22	·24	·08	·12	49	49	49	50	48	47	47	46	48·4	51	1·025*
Means														

* It may be right to observe here, that the density of the sea, as given in this column of the abstract, is at best but a near approximation. Through the kindness of Professor Fyfe, of King's College, Aberdeen, at the conclusion of the voyage, I ascertained that the instrument by which the observations were made had an error of about ·0013, which requires to be added uniformly to the whole series. I did not, however, deem it necessary to apply this correction, for the reason that the difference thus effected in the observations would not in the slightest degree affect the chief feature to be noticed, namely, the extremely regular manner in which, in the polar regions at least, temperatures below 39° cause the precipitation of the saline ingredients of sea-water.

ABSTRACT OF THE METEOROLOGICAL JOURNAL KEPT ON BOARD THE DISCOVERY SHIP ISABEL, CAPT. INGLEFIELD, R.N., NOVEMBER, 1852.—*North Atlantic.*

Dates.	WINDS.		WEATHER.		Clouds, according to Howard's nomenclature.	Position at Noon.		
	Direction.	Estimated Force.	A.M.	P.M.		Lat.	Long.	Names of Places.
						° ′	° ′	
1	N.E. to N.W.	4–2–8	*m.o.r.* : *v.b.c.q.p.*		K.C.	58 54	20 31	In the east side of the N. Atlantic.
2	N.W. to S.W.	8–5	v.b.c.q.p. : *v.b.c.*		K.	58 52	15 46	
*3	S.W.	6–9	v.b.c.l.g.q.		CK.K.	58 56	10 0	
4	S. to S.E.	9–3	v.o.c.q.p.r.		K.C.N.	59 0	5 48	
†5	S.S.E.	3–11	*m.v.b.c.r.p.q.*		K.N.	...	...	Dunnet Head.
‡6	S.W.	8–4	v.b.c.l.m.r.o.		K.N.	...	...	In Stromness harbour.
7	S.E. to S.W.	7–8	v.b. : c.r.m.		K.N.	...	...	
8	W.	5–8	v.b.c.r.p.q.		CK.N.	...	...	
9	N.W.	6–8	v.b.c.p.q.r.		K.N.	...	...	Ham Sound.
§10	N. to N.E.	8–6	v.b.c.q.p.		K.N.	...	...	Peterhead Bay.
11	N.N.E.	5–8	v.b.c. : v.o.c.		K.C.N.	...	...	Bell Rock.
12	E.S.E.	8–9	v.b.c. : v.b.c.q.p.		K.C.N.	...	...	Frith of Forth.
13	E.S.E.	8–4	v.b.c. : q.m.r.		K.N.			
**14	E.S.E.	3–8	*m.o.r.*		...	...	...	St. Margaret's Hope.
15	E.S.E.	10–8	*m.o.r.*		...	...	...	
16	VBLE., E.	6–1	m.o.d.		...			
17	VBLE., S.E.	1–5	m.o.d.r. : v.b.c.		CK.			
18	S. to W.	7	v.b.c.		CS.CK.	...	...	Off Bass Island.
19	W. to S.	7–6	v.b.c.		CS.CK.	...	...	Flamborough Head.
20	S.W. to S.E.	6–3	*v.b.* : *m.o.r.*		S.CS.	...	...	Dudgeon L.
21	S.W. to S.E.	3–1	m.o.r.		..	...	...	Off Winterton.
22	NORTH.	4–7	m.o.c. : v.b.c.		K.	...	....	Thames Sea-Reach.
Means								

* Flashes of lightning; Aurora Borealis in the northern and western sky. Peculiar murky haze on the eastern horizon.

† Halo around the moon at 1 A.M., deficient in its lower part (E.S.E.); murky haze over all the sky, which however does not obscure the stars.

‡ Tremendous gale.

§ *Cumulus* and *Nimbus* clouds, loading the atmosphere, and drifting before the wind.

** Densely loaded atmosphere, mist, and rain; tops of the high hills on the south side of the Frith of Forth enveloped in a hoary mantle of snow and mist.

APPENDIX.

A Table, shewing the indications of the Standard Barometer, and of two Aneroid Barometers, every Day at Noon, during the month of September.

Dates.	Standard Barometer.		Aneroid Barometers.				Difference, as observed between the Standard and the Aneroids.	
	Bar.	Ther.	5918.	Ther.	4784.	Ther.	5918.	4784.
	Inches.	°	Inches.	°	Inches.	°	Inches.	Inches.
1	29·62	52	29·65	49	29·71	53	+ ·03	+ ·09
2	·54	72	·58	68	·63	72	+ ·04	+ ·09
3	·83	78	·86	74	·91	78	+ ·03	+ ·08
4	·83	66	·82	60	·91	65	— ·01	+ ·08
5	·71	70	·74	68	·78	72	+ ·03	+ ·07
6	·67	78	·71	75	·75	80	+ ·04	+ ·08
7	·85	70	·92	63	·96	68	+ ·07	+ ·11
8	30·04	51	30·06	47	30·10	52	+ ·02	+ ·06
9	29·88	45	29·93	42	29·96	45	+ ·05	+ ·05
10	·82	52	·93	46	·96	48	+ ·01	+ ·14
11	30·18	46	30·25	40	30·28	43	+ ·07	+ ·10
12	·18	55	·26	49	·28	51	+ ·08	+ ·10
13	29·97	55	·01	52	·05	54	+ ·04	+ ·08
14	·97	70	·01	67	·05	70	+ ·04	+ ·08
15	·80	66	29·84	58	29·87	62	+ ·04	+ ·07
16	30·35	77	30·40	75	30·44	78	+ ·05	+ ·09
17	·22	56	·26	51	·30	54	+ ·04	+ ·08
18	29·90	57	29·96	51	·00	54	+ ·06	+ ·10
19	·87	66	·93	62	29·96	64	+ ·06	+ ·09
20	·67	47	·72	42	·76	45	+ ·05	+ ·09
21	·77	43	·81	44	·86	46	+ ·04	+ ·09
22	·87	56	·92	51	·96	53	+ ·05	+ ·09
23	30·00	51	30·03	46	30·06	45	+ ·03	+ ·06
24	29·78	54	29·81	50	29·84	52	+ ·03	+ ·06
25	·20	43	·24	40	·27	41	+ ·04	+ ·07
26	30·06	41	·98	38	30·04	35	— ·08	— ·02
27	29·79	44	·79	48	29·83	46	·00	+ ·04
28	·67	46	·63	42	·67	48	— ·04	·00
29	30·04	51	30·08	49	30·12	43	+ ·04	+ ·08
30	·25	67	·27	62	·22	57	+ ·02	+ ·03

Note.—The two Aneroids (Dent's) were placed, one on each side of the Standard Barometer, about two feet above the level of the sea. They ranged from 27·50 to 31, and had spirit of wine thermometers. The observations are uncorrected, it being unnecessary for mere comparison to enter into such minute detail.

PROCEEDINGS

OF

COMMANDER E. A. INGLEFIELD, R. N.,

COMMANDING THE PRIVATE SCREW STEAM-VESSEL ISABEL,

ON A

VOYAGE OF ARCTIC DISCOVERY.

Letter from Commander Inglefield, R.N., *to the Secretary of the Admiralty.*

9, Portsea-place, Connaught-square,

Sir, 21 June, 1852.

The Isabel screw schooner, of 170 tons, and thirty-horse power, doubled, fitted and provisioned for a five years' cruise, having, through the failure of Captain Beatson's intended expedition, been thrown upon the hands of Lady Franklin, and that lady having made offer to me of her vessel (since the reply of their Lordships) on the condition that I should carry her by whatever route may appear most likely to obtain some information of the missing expedition, I beg to lay before you, for the information of my Lords Commissioners of the Admiralty, this proposal; and,

First, to solicit their Lordships' approval and permission to accept her Ladyship's offer, and to grant me leave of absence for that purpose.

Secondly, to petition, that should their Lordships be disposed to approve the undertaking, they will grant me such assistance, to be paid for by myself, which the

P

Dockyard at Woolwich could immediately supply
towards some few internal arrangements still required
to complete her, and which, if done at a private yard,
might occasion a prejudicial delay.

Briefly, my views in undertaking this expedition are,
to accomplish a perfect examination of the west coast
of Baffin Bay and Labrador; and the season, from recent
accounts from Copenhagen, having every appearance of
being favourable, I am most desirous to lose no time in
visiting that coast, from which, if the story of the brig
Renovation is to be credited, those icebergs probably
drifted, on which the vessels were seen, and though such
ships may not be those of Sir John Franklin's squadron,
the cause of humanity will be furthered as much, by
endeavouring to assist their crews, as those of Her
Majesty's exploring vessels.

Notwithstanding my own feelings, and that of most
Arctic voyagers well qualified to express their convic-
tions as to the fate of Sir John Franklin and his gallant
comrades, I cannot allow myself to undertake the
enterprise, excepting with the full and entire approval
of the Board of Admiralty; for having six times volunteered for Arctic service, and being still most anxiously
looking for either promotion or employment, I am very
unwilling to place myself out of the reach of their
Lordships; but as it is the determination of Lady
Franklin to send this vessel in any case, my own san-
guine hopes as to the safety of Sir John, together with
the earnest desire to devote myself to the search (though
at my own expense for the wages of the crew, and
without any chance of remuneration); all these com-
bine and incline me to accept the offer rather than it
should be said no officer was to be found who would

undertake this voyage in the cause of humanity ; and should I refuse it, it is understood the vessel will be immediately given to some whaling captain, who might be looked upon as more hardy and enterprising than any, his fellows of Her Majesty's Navy.

I am, &c.,

(signed)   E. A. INGLEFIELD,

Commander.

Letter from the Secretary of the Admiralty to Commander Inglefield.

Sir,   Admiralty, 22 June, 1852.

I have received and laid before my Lords your letter of the 21st instant, requesting the sanction of their Lordships to your taking the command of the " Isabel" screw schooner, belonging to Lady Franklin, with a view to proceed to the Polar regions in search of the missing expedition under Sir John Franklin ; and I am commanded to acquaint you, that their Lordships have no objection to your taking command of the vessel named, if you should think proper to do so ; and they will grant you one year's leave of absence for the purpose, or such further leave as you may require.

And my Lords will have no objection to order any refit to the vessel, or fittings to be made good at Woolwich Dockyard that may be required, on the understanding that the expense incurred is to be repaid.

I am, &c.,

(Signed)   J. H. HAY,

Pro. Sec.

P 2

Letter from Mr. J. H. Hay (for the Secretary of the Admiralty) to the Commodore Superintendent of Woolwich Dockyard.

Admiralty, 22 June, 1852.

Commodore Superintendent, Woolwich,

Commander Inglefield having applied to my Lords for permission for any repairs or fittings that may be required to the Isabel screw schooner, to be made good at Woolwich Dockyard, my Lords have been pleased to consent to the request, on the understanding that the expense thereof be repaid.

I am, &c.,

(Signed)   J. H. HAY,

Pro. Sec.

———

Letter from Commander Inglefield to the Secretary of the Admiralty.

Screw Discovery Vessel, Isabel, off the Nore,

Sir,   5 July, 1852.

Having left Greenhithe in tow of the Lightning, I cannot take my departure without once more expressing my sincere gratitude to my Lords Commissioners of the Admiralty for the invaluable assistance I have received at Her Majesty's Dockyard at Woolwich; and I feel, moreover, that it would be unbecoming of me to leave on the adventurous voyage I am commencing, without giving their Lordships a short outline of my intended route.

I hope to reach the northern extremity of Baffin Bay, touching only at Holsteinburg, without any further check than such as I may find in crossing Melville Bay ; but should I be disappointed in obtaining a sufficiently high latitude this season to examine Smith and Jones Sound, I shall then cross (if practicable) to the west coast of Baffin Bay, and commence an examination southward along that shore; I shall endeavour to return before the winter sets in to England; but should I fail in this, will hope to communicate with Sir Edward Belcher across the land from Jones Sound.

I have once more to request you will offer their Lordships my sincere thanks for their assistance, and express my earnest hope that, as by their Lordships' letter to me, I infer that it was only on account of there being no available vessel that they refused my request to be towed beyond Peterhead, I may still trust their Lordships will permit the Lightning to take me some small distance to the westward, as to such an incalculably valuable aid I may thus impute the whole success of my undertaking, for the lateness of the season otherwise might prevent my doing more this year than entering the ice.

I am, &c.,

(Signed)   E. A. INGLEFIELD.

Commander.

Letter from the Secretary of the Admiralty to Commander Inglefield.

Sir,   Admiralty, 7 July, 1852.

With reference to your letter of the 5th instance, requesting that Her Majesty's steam vessel, Light-

ning, may be ordered to tow the Isabel beyond
Peterhead, I am to acquaint you that they cannot com-
ply with your request.

I am, &c.,

(Signed)   A. STAFFORD.

---

*Letter from Commander Inglefield to the Secretary of
the Admiralty.*

Screw Discovery Vessel, Isabel, 12 August, 1852.

Goodhaven, Disko, Greenland.

Sir,

The assistance I have received in so many ways from
the Board of Admiralty, in equipping my little vessel
for her Arctic voyage, induces me to suppose their
Lordships will be pleased to learn I have so far advanced
on my voyage, and that the squadron under Sir Edward
Belcher passed this port on the 12th of June, having
left it on the 10th, and finding the Waigatt Passage
blocked with ice, returned southward to take the open
bay.

I shall sail in a few hours, having only put into Goodhaven to make good some losses sustained in a gale off
Farewell.

I am now (from the favourable appearance of the
season, and the opinion of those here, as to the state of
the ice northward), determined upon proceeding direct
to Smith Sound.

No ships having been seen returning southward from Melville Bay, it is presumed that they have been successful in making an early north passage.

I am, &c.,

(Signed)   E. A. INGLEFIELD,

Commander, R.N.

Letter from Commander Inglefield to the Secretary of the Admiralty.

Screw Discovery Vessel Isabel,

off Cape Adair, West Coast of Baffin Bay,

Sir,   15 September, 1852.

Having, since my last communication to you, completed that part of my voyage in which I undertook the examination of the northern extremity of Baffin Bay, in search of the missing vessels under the command of Sir John Franklin, and presuming upon the interest which my Lords Commissioners of the Admiralty have taken in the exploration of those and the adjacent shores, I take advantage of a vessel bound to England to acquaint their Lordships of my discoveries in those high latitudes, and herewith enclose a tracing from my track chart, which I beg you will state to their Lordships, must not be considered at present more than an eye sketch, though the necessary data for a more perfect outline is obtained, and in progress of formation into what I doubt not will prove a correct outline.

2. From Disko Island, where I last addressed myself

to you, I proceeded to Uppernivik, there to obtain an interpreter, and purchase dogs; the former could not be procured, the latter was readily supplied me.

3. From Uppernivik I proceeded northward, crossing Melville Bay with little difficulty. At Cape York I passed through a great quantity of loose ice, composed of large bergs and floe pieces; the weather, however, was sufficiently easy to admit of my steaming through, and on the morning of the 22nd of August I reached the great glacier of Petowak. Becalmed off this gigantic ice formation, which extends for upwards of four miles inland and a mile to seaward, with a smooth unbroken sloping surface, I got so closely in that voices were heard shouting from the beach, and soon natives were descried coming down the face of the glacier and two small ravines adjoining. On proceeding to the shore, with some difficulty in getting through the young bay ice, which had commenced rapidly to form, I reached a sandy cove, where after a little delay in calming the apprehensions of the Esquimaux by signs and a few presents, I endeavoured to obtain from them information as to the position of north Omenak, and if possible a pilot. A woman, who appeared more intelligent than the rest of the party, drew upon the snow an outline of the coast and the position of the settlement known now as the reputed scene of the murder of Franklin and his people, by the statement of Adam Beck. These people seemed the very opposite. extreme of those seen last year at Cape York; they are robust, strong, healthy individuals, and well supplied with children; they impressed me with a notion that they had not before seen Europeans; their immoderate laughter when I had assured them of our good intent,

and surprise at our clothing, boats, &c., led me to this conviction.

4. Sailing northward, I reached Cape Athol on the morning of the 23rd, and falling calm, I took advantage of that day to steam right round the Bay, within pistol-shot of the shore.

5. The settlement of N. Omenak, which I readily found in a deep bight on the north side of Wolstenholme Sound, was deserted, but evidently only for the season, as the store of blubber, winter clothing, and flesh which I discovered in my search for traces of the missing vessels, I think, proved. Every great hut and store-house was closely overhauled, and a large heap of heavy stones, apparently without any use, was pulled down, and a foot deep dug into the frozen earth; the pile consisted of bones of seals, walrus, whale, birds, and fish, but no trace of anything European could be discovered. I may add that I was induced to examine this cairn from the statement of Mr. Abernethy, my chief mate, who was in the same vessel with Adam Beck when he related that the bones of the murdered crew were concealed in a cairn of this description. No traces discovered, and some observations made to fix more correctly the position of Wolstenholme and Saunders Island with that of two others before unnoticed, and three incorrectly laid down, off the entrance of Granville Bay; I proceeded against a heavy gale from the N.W. (which brought vast quantities of ice to the southward), towards Cape Parry, and on the afternoon of the 25th, after having been blown back three times, we entered Whale Sound.

6. Twenty-five miles inside this opening in the coast, a settlement of natives was observed and visited; I

remarked the same fear at our approach, but like means adopted as previously, soon allayed their apprehensions. A mile from the spot where I landed we found the summer habitations of these people, who were as strong, healthy, and vigorous as any I have seen on the coast ; an ample store of blubber and flesh, laid by in their winter under-ground hovels, proved that want was, for this season at least, unknown to them.

7. Neither here nor at Petowak were kyaks seen, but numerous dogs and sledges, somewhat different in form to those observed southward.

8. A knife which I obtained, with " B. Wilson, cast steel," on the blade, and having been apparently a table-knife, but mounted in a rude ivory handle, made from the tooth of a sea unicorn, an axe without mark, a tin canister, and several pieces of steel curiously converted into a knife, with some rope, were the only articles I observed of European manufacture, but I did not attach much importance to them, as the nomadic habits of the natives on this coast may easily account for the manner in which they may have been acquired.

8. Before returning to the boat, I ascended an eminence of nearly 1000 feet, and from its summit beheld that the north side of the Sound was composed of a group of islands, some of considerable dimensions.

A rapid sketch made on the spot will convey some notion of the appearance of the Sound at this point.

10. On returning to my vessel at 12 P.M., which I found at some distance from where I left her, (owing to her having struck heavily twice on a sunken rock in the middle of the bight), I steered away on a course to pass out on the north side of the largest island, and between

that and a smaller one; to these two islands I have presumed to give the names of his Grace the First Lord, and Sir Thomas Herbert; the next was called Tyrconnel Island.

11. In the settlement one mile and a-half astern, I was much surprised to observe two small openings (so marked at least on the charts) to be extensive inlets, opening away to the northward and north-eastward; the sky beautifully illumined by the rising sun, would readily have defined the land, though as far as the eye could reach, an unbroken horizon met the gaze, and no sign of ice or obstruction into an open strait or inland sea could be detected.

This inlet I named after Sir Roderick Murchison.

12. Nothing but the sense of my duty to Lady Franklin prevented my searching the course of this fair strait, through which, owing to a calm that occurred at 4 A.M., I estimated the current to be setting eastward $3\frac{1}{2}$ miles an hour.

13. No traces having been met with of the missing expedition, I felt that Franklin was no longer to be sought for here, and thus I determined to take advantage of the evidently open state of the ice, and dash boldly at once to the northward, in the direction of Smith Sound.

14. Cape Alexander I reached at midnight of the 26th, rounding it under sail and steam within half musket shot of the shore, having a depth of 145 fathoms, sand and small broken shells.

We narrowly escaped falling on board of a large iceberg, owing to the wind heading us round the point. Nothing resembling a cairn could be detected on either this headland or a curiously shaped island on the south side of it; for though midnight, it was as light as day, and the sun was just gilding the northern sky behind the extreme north point, which in honour to His Royal Highness' birthday I named Cape Albert.

We had no sooner fairly opened the Sound than I involuntarily exclaimed, this must lead into the great Polynia of the Russians; and as the eye strained forward into the clear expanse of apparently open water, which now occupied from seven to eight points of the compass due north of our position, I could not but admit to my own mind that a great sea was beyond.

15. The strait marked so narrow on our charts (by measurement on the morrow) I found to be about thirty-six miles across; and now I pushed eagerly on to a further view of this noble inlet.

16. The natural snow-clad aspect of the bleak cliffs that surround the head of the bay, seemed changed by the presence of a more genial clime, the side of Cape Alexander itself being streaked with bright green grasses and moss, and the neighbouring hills to the northward were black instead of snow-capped, evidently too of secondary formation,

17. The west coast of this new sea which I had now entered, trended away to the N.W., as the coast grew still more to the eastward, and a high range of mountains, which I named the Prince of Wales range, terminated the western shore in a bluff, which I called Victoria Head.

18. Here the outline of coast ceased; for though I reached on noon of the 27th, latitude 78°; the 28th, nothing but loose ice could be espied from aloft beyond the two Capes, Frederick VII. and Victoria.

19. A few icebergs and loose ice setting with ourselves to the northward, at the rate of about three
miles an hour (a current which I detected, during the
whole of our run up the coast from Wolstenholme
Sound, and which seemed to separate itself by an
eddy into the Murchison inlet), together with a fast
land-floe, extending 'about twelve miles from the
western shore enclosing Cape Isabella, were all the
obstructions which presented themselves to our onward
course into this great Polar Sea; and had not circumstances over which I could have no control, and which
I may perhaps term providential, defied my further
progress, I should have been allured by the prospect
before me to penetrate yet further north.

20. Having satisfactorily obtained the latitude at
noon, which I called my officers to witness, and by
sights for my chronometers at nine, a tolerable longitude, my attention was turned towards effecting a
landing, the better to observe the variation and dip,
whilst a cairn was erecting to mark our visit, and note
that the British Flag was the first to be carried into
this unknown sea. By the time the people had dined,
a still further advance had been made, assisted mate-
rially by the northerly set, but the breeze had now
freshened to a strong gale, and going against the
current, had set up a sea that constrained my officers to
advise me against attempting to land in the light short
boat we possessed.

They declared in their opinion it would be risking
the lives of the people, and anxious as I was to put
foot on these newly-found shores, I felt bound to
accept their advice, and now, whilst seeking this landing
place in a bay to leeward of an island I named after

my friend Lord Hatherton, a gale had commenced with such fury that we were fairly blown out of the strait; and ere six hours elapsed we were hove to in a tempest of wind and snow (which lasted thirty-six hours) under a close-reefed fore topsail.

21. On the morning of the 29th it moderated, and in trying to hug the west shore, with the view of exploring its coasts, we were drifted into the lee pack, which girt the western side of the head of Baffin Bay, extending about twenty miles to leeward.

The slight breeze and heavy swells which had set us on, soon placed the ship in a most dangerous position; a leak in our boiler had put the engine for the time *hors de combat*, and I began to contemplate that in a few hours we should be firmly fixed in this extensive pack.

Observing the rudder splintering, from the crushing pressure of the ice, I ordered the boiler to be hastily secured and the steam got up, as our last resource, and by God's mercy, after several hours of anxiety and hard labour on the part of all on board, we were extricated from our difficulties, and steamed out to seaward.

22. I determined now upon following down the west coast, as near as I could, to Cobourg Island and then passing through Glacier Strait to proceed up Jones Sound.

This I accomplished, passing up into the Sound on the 31st of August, and beating against a fresh westerly breeze, assisted by a strong set, reached longitude 84°, from whence the coast suddenly turned away in a N.W. direction, the south shore trending rather northerly; but as far as the eye could scan in the west horizon, no land could be discovered though great masses of ice were driving rapidly down.

23. No traces of our missing countrymen could be espied, and the evening of the 1st of September setting in with thick fog, accompanied by a stiff gale from the westward, and snow-drift, the inhospitable appearance, which seemed to defy the foot of man, and to prove the impossibility of finding shelter for a winter season, these combined to warn me that prudence dictated our return, and indeed, as no examination could be made in such thick weather as now set in, the object of my visit would be defeated if I ran blindly on as far as the ice now seen to windward would admit, I therefore ran over to the south shore and towards the eastward, examining as closely as I could each point and bend in the coast, but no cairns, no mark could be observed.

24. Several additions and alterations in the chart were made, and passing through the Lady Anne Strait, by midnight I was abreast of Cape Parker. Here we were suddenly beset by floe pieces upwards of twenty feet in thickness, and by them hemmed in on every side, within a mile of the shore.

A breeze from the N.W. would have sealed our fate in all probability for a winter in this pack, or wreck on Cape Parker, but aided by the powerful arm of steam, we succeeded with much labour in boring out, and by noon of the 2nd had secured a good offing amongst "brash ice" drifting off Cape Horsburgh.

25. I now resolved, before entering upon my search down the western coasts of Baffin Bay and Labrador, to take advantage of the still open appearance of the season to visit Beechey Island, and obtaining, for the information of their Lordships, the most recent accounts

of Sir Edward Belcher's expedition, supply him in return with the mail I had brought from England (our latest dates only eight weeks old), and above all, an outline of my discoveries and a tracing from my track chart, which, as his orders had reference to a part of the coast I had explored, might prove of some use to him.

26. Light adverse winds prevented my reaching Her Majesty's depôt ship North Star before the morning of the 7th September, when I entered Erebus and Terror Bay, and finding it well open anchored for a few hours.

27. From Commander Pullen I obtained much information relative to the expedition, but as the Prince Albert had sailed only a fortnight previously, he had little else than duplicates of the despatches forwarded by her to charge me with, and as nothing official can be communicated by me that will not have appeared in those despatches, I will not intrude farther upon their Lordships' attention than to acquaint them that I am now vigorously prosecuting the search down the west shore of Baffin Bay, touching when practicable, and erecting cairns, at night firing guns and throwing up rockets.

28. I shall hope, under Providence, to reach England without incurring the heavy expense to myself of remaining out for the winter.

29. With this view I return the despatches from Commander Pullen, but as I cannot forsee what may befall the ship in the course of our explorations on the dangerous coast of Labrador, I deem it my duty to seize this opportunity of communicating to their Lordships the result of my labours, and I trust the exertions I

have made will meet their approval, and set at rest the public mind as to the possibility of finding traces of the missing squadron on the shores I have visited.

About half only of my fuel is expended, owing to the strictest economy, and thus I trust to making careful examinations to the southward.

30. October 22.—Thus far I had prepared my letter, in the expectation of falling in with whalers off Home Bay; but upon reaching the Hecla and Griper Bank, my progress was arrested by a vast body of ice, which appearing to be toggled on to the shore by a line of icebergs grounded on the shoals, stretched far away to seaward, and carried me into longitude 61½°, ere I could get away south. Two days and a night in the pack at last enabled me to get through.

31. On the 22nd, we had run 120 miles to the southward; but the morning of the 23rd was ushered in with the most tremendous gale (from the S.E.) I ever witnessed; for six days we lay to under a storm sail, occasionally sighting the land, or vast bergs driving rapidly past us, through the mist and spray. Our water being now nearly expended (having purposed to refit and water in the Clyde), and being now upon the allowance of a pint per man, and the ship, moreover, much disabled, I was compelled (on the weather moderating) to take the first harbour; accordingly, I ran into the Hunde Islands on the 2nd of October for that purpose.

32. On the 7th we sailed, to encounter another gale from the S.W., which lasted till the 10th, and then only moderating to freshen into a still more violent one from the N.E.

33. Before this, we scudded for two days, making over

Q

to the west shore, in the hopes of gaining Cumberland Inlet, where I intended to winter, and possibly complete the search from where I had left it, by means of my dog-sledges.

The tremendous following sea breaking high over the stern of our little vessel, and occasionally deluging the decks, obliged us to keep certain sail on the ship, and we had now scudded too long to heave to ; at this juncture, running past the point I wished to make, my ice-masters came to me with their advice, that I should make no farther attempt to reach the coast at this advanced period of the season, and with such boisterous weather.

Mr. Manson, who has been employed many years in the whaling trade, assured me, that the dangers of this coast could only be safely approached in moderate weather, and strongly urged my relinquishing the attempt.

34. Having waited two days after this advice, in the hope that the weather might moderate, I decided upon returning to England, and am now on my homeward voyage, having remained within the Arctic Circle exactly two months later than the expedition of last year ; and (having reached it three months later) have, nevertheless, accomplished (independent of sailing) 1,473 miles (under steam), bringing home with me still sixty-six tons of fuel.

35. I cannot speak too highly of the advantages of the high-pressure engine, which working at forty pounds on the square inch, has given ample opportunities of testing its utility ; no difference in temperature affecting its working, though consuming patent fuel, with which the upper deck had been paved and exposed to

the weather, salt-water and trampling on for two months previous to its use.

36. My large chart being now finished with the track round Baffin Bay, and the discoveries I have made, comprising 600 miles of new coast line correctly laid down, I do not now enclose the eye-sketch before alluded to ; but shall take the earliest opportunity of waiting on their Lordships with the same, and numerous sketches of the unknown coasts I have explored.

Apologising for intruding at such length upon the time of my Lords Commissioners,

I have, &c.,

(Signed)   E. A. INGLEFIELD,

Commander, R.N.

Letter from the President and Vice-President of the Royal Geographical Society to his Grace the Duke of Northumberland.

Royal Geographical Society,

My Lord Duke,   12 December, 1852.

Conscious of the value which geographers and the public have attributed to the recent Arctic researches of Commander Inglefield, R.N., we venture to submit to your Grace a notice of those services, which may, we trust, move the Lords Commissioners of the Admiralty to promote that distinguished officer.

The new official chart of the Polar Regions shows how many errors of former delineation of the headlands, gulfs, and inlands of Baffin Bay have been corrected by him, and how he has obtained entirely new data respecting Smith Sound, which go far to settle the belief, that Franklin must have taken the route of Wellington Channel.

Acquainted as we were with the very untoward circumstances under which Commander Inglefield volunteered to take the command of the small private vessel the Isabel, and seeing the energy with which, in overcoming all difficulties, he carried out the wishes of Lady Franklin and the subscribers to the expedition, we might well admire results which, in the words of the first of living authorities on such a subject, Sir Edward Parry, "have placed Commander Inglefield among the most distinguished of our Arctic navigators."

Addressing your Grace and the Board, in our capacity as members of the Royal Geographical Society, we consider ourselves precluded from fortifying our application by any reference to the services of Commander Inglefield in the ordinary duties of his professional career, but we may state that the selection of him for the command of an exploring expedition was indeed founded on our knowledge of the character of those previous services.

We confine ourselves, however, to the fact, that expectations founded on that knowledge have been more than realized by the zeal and ability which he has displayed, and by the value to science of the results he obtained.

It is specially, therefore, as geographers, that we address your Grace and the Board of Admiralty, in the hope that as the recent explorations of Commander Inglefield have been very generally approved, you will reward an officer who has employed his best energies,

and expended much of his own pecuniary means in so
noble a cause.

We have, &c.

(Signed)   RODERICK MURCHISON,
President, R. G. S.

EGERTON ELLESMERE,
Vice-President, R. G. S.

————

Report on Commander INGLEFIELD'S *Arctic Voyage.*

Admiralty, 17 December, 1852.

Sharing in the universal feeling about the fate of
Franklin's party, Commander Inglefield eagerly accepted the gift of the Isabel, of 149 tons, in order to
join in search for them.   Marvellously soon equipped,
he steered for Davis Strait; pushed forward through
the ice; passing by the tempting opening of Murchison
Strait, and succeeded in penetrating into the heart of
Smith Sound, which, as well as the former opening,
he has proved to lead into the Polar Basin.

This may well be called a valuable discovery, for
Baffin merely saw a break in the coast, and Ross and
Parry could only just perceive the looming of the
mountains at the distance of ninety miles.   Murchison
Strait was likewise another important geographical
discovery, for Whale Sound, with which it is con-
nected, was supposed to be only a deep fiord, whereas
it now appears to be a wide passage, and to be the
limits of the continent of Greenland.

In the third place, the ice having prevented Captain
Austin from entering Jones Sound, but which seemed

to him to be only a deep bay, now turns out to be another channel to the northward, through the great cluster of Parry Islands.

With respect to Commander Inglefield's chart, which shows the configurations of both shores 140 miles further north than had been effected by any former navigator, when we consider the size of his vessel, and the constant demands upon his time, as he seldom quitted the deck, day or night, we may well be surprised at the accuracy of its details, and the correctness with which it is borne out by his journal and observation books; all of which have been submitted for examination to this office.

A change of weather having forced him to retire from Baffin Bay, and undaunted by the approach of winter, though unfurnished with the means of passing it in an Arctic climate, he had the generous boldness to run up Barrow Strait, in order to offer his surplus of provisions to Sir Edward Belcher's ships, and to bring home intelligence of their then state to Government and to their numerous friends.

All this has been performed in four months, and all accomplished without the drawback of a single accident; every obstacle having been overcome by his persevering energy, and every vain temptation resisted by his singleness of purpose, altogether forming, in my estimation, one of the most extraordinary voyages on record.

(Signed)   F. BEAUFORT.

Letter from the Secretary of the Admiralty to Commander
INGLEFIELD.

Sir, Admiralty, 20 December, 1852.

With reference to your letter of 15th September last, off Cape Adair, reporting your proceedings in the schooner Isabel, in pursuit of further traces of Sir John Franklin, and of your return to communicate with the station at Beechey Island, I am commanded to acquaint you, that my Lords Commissioners of the Admiralty approve of the spirit which prompted you in making that visit, and their Lordships having this day had before them the observations of the hydrographer, on the discoveries you made in your voyage, my Lords acknowledge with satisfaction the enterprize and energy you have displayed in your late research, and although your endeavours to discover traces of the missing expedition have not been rewarded with success, my Lords consider that they do credit to yourself, and that your voyage is not without importance in its geographical results.

(Signed) W. A. B. HAMILTON.

———

Letter from the Secretary of the Admiralty to the President
of the Royal Geographical Society.

Sir, Admiralty, 24 December, 1852.

Having laid before my Lords Commissioners of the Admiralty the letter addressed by yourself and the Vice-President of the Royal Geographical Society to his Grace the Duke of Northumberland, recommending Commander Inglefield for reward for his services in the Arctic Seas, I am commanded by their Lordships to send you a copy of their letter of approbation, addressed to Commander Inglefield, and which will show the opinion entertained of that officer.

I am, &c.

(Signed)   **W. A. B. HAMILTON.**

PRINTED BY HARRISON AND SONS,
St. Martin's Lane, and Orchard Street, Westminster.

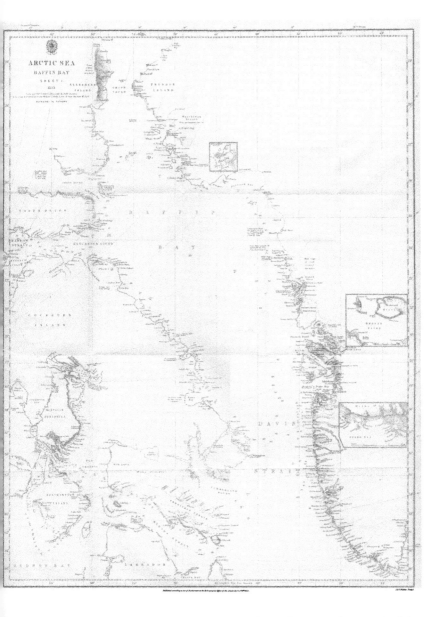

The material originally positioned here is too large for reproduction in this reissue. A PDF can be downloaded from the web address given on page iv of this book, by clicking on 'Resources Available'.

For EU product safety concerns, contact us at Calle de José Abascal, 56–1°,
28003 Madrid, Spain or eugpsr@cambridge.org.

www.ingramcontent.com/pod-product-compliance
Ingram Content Group UK Ltd.
Pitfield, Milton Keynes, MK11 3LW, UK
UKHW010342140625
459647UK00010B/770